Mag. Claudia Lichtenwagner

SMILE 2
Grammar

Englisch Übungsbuch für die
2. Klasse Mittelschule / AHS

Von Claudia Lichtenwagner bisher im G&G Verlag erschienen:

Smile Listening Comprehensions 1 (978-3-7074-1978-8)
Smile Listening Comprehensions 2 (978-3-7074-2061-6)
Smile Listening Comprehensions 3 (978-3-7074-2184-2)
Smile Listening Comprehensions 4 (978-3-7074-2187-3)

Smile 1 Grammar (978-3-7074-1306-9)
Smile 2 Grammar (978-3-7074-1307-6)
Smile 3 Grammar (978-3-7074-1308-3)
Smile 4 Grammar (978-3-7074-1309-0)

Smile Reading Comprehensions 1 (978-3-7074-1354-0)
Smile Reading Comprehensions 2 (978-3-7074-1508-7)
Smile Reading Comprehensions 3 (978-3-7074-1624-4)
Smile Reading Comprehensions 4 (978-3-7074-1846-0)

Smile Matura-Trainer Speaking Competences (978-3-7074-2080-7)

Sourire 1 (978-3-7074-1310-6)
Sourire 2 (978-3-7074-1311-3)
Sourire 3 (978-3-7074-1312-0)
Sourire 4 (978-3-7074-1313-7)
Sourire 5 (978-3-7074-1314-4)

Dieses Werk ist für den Schul- und Unterrichtsgebrauch bestimmt.

Es darf gemäß § 42 (3) des Urheberrechtsgesetzes auch für den eigenen Unterrichtsgebrauch nicht vervielfältigt werden.

SMILE – die erfolgreichste Englisch-Lernhilfenreihe jetzt auch online auf

- Über 6.500 interaktive Übungen zu allen Grammatik-Themen
- Wiederholung, Testvorbereitung und Hausaufgaben mit automatisierten Auswertungen zur Selbstüberprüfung
- https://eduactive.at/smile

Smile

www.ggverlag.at

ISBN 978-3-7074-1307-6

39. Auflage 2025

Druck und Bindung: Brüder Glöckler, Wöllersdorf

© 2010 G&G Verlagsgesellschaft mbH, Frankgasse 4, 1090 Wien
produktsicherheit@ggverlag.at
Alle Rechte vorbehalten. Jede Art der Vervielfältigung, auch die des auszugsweisen Nachdrucks, der fotomechanischen Wiedergabe, der Einspeicherung und Verarbeitung in elektronische Systeme sowie Text- und Data-Mining sind ohne ausdrückliche Zustimmung des Verlages gesetzlich verboten.
Gedruckt auf Papier aus geprüfter nachhaltiger Forstwirtschaft.

VORWORT

Liebe Schülerin, lieber Schüler!

Dieser zweite Band der erfolgreichen SMILE-Übungsreihe behandelt wichtige Grammatikkapitel aus dem zweiten Lernjahr.
Durch die den vielen Übungssätzen vorangestellten Grammatikregeln und dem "Key" im Anhang ist das Buch sowohl zum Selbststudium als auch als Hilfsmittel für den Unterricht geeignet.

Im "Key" findest du gelegentlich Hinweise auf SMILE I (mit Angabe der Seitennummer) bzw. auf die im jeweiligen Fall zutreffende Grammatikregel. Sind bei Übungssätzen mehrere Lösungen möglich, so sind diese auch im "Key" angeführt. Neue Vokabeln sind mit der im Buch geltenden deutschen Bedeutung vor dem "Key" zusammengestellt.

Ich wünsche dir recht viel Freude beim Üben!

Prof. Mag. Claudia Lichtenwagner

CONTENTS

page

Regular and irregular past forms	1
Negation and question in past tense	2
Tenses (present simple, present progressive, going to future, past tense)	4
Asking and explaining the way	5
Modal verbs	6
Should / should not / ought to / oughtn't to	12
What about? How about?	13
Like, would like, want, need	13
To, too	14
Translation (*How about, what about, like, would like, want, need, too*)	15
During, while	17
Some	18
Any	19
One, ones	24
Every, each, all	26
As, when	31
Comparison of adjectives	33
As ... as, not so/as ... as, the same ... as, than, less, fewer, a bit, far, more	38
Will-future	45
Going to-future	47
The adverb	52
Adjective or adverb	55
Prepositional phrases	58
Condition: *What would you do if ...?*	62
Conjunctions	63
Present perfect tense simple	68
For, since	72
Present perfect or past tense	73
Possessive pronouns: *mine, yours, his, hers, its, ours, theirs*	78
Past tense progressive	79
Lots (of), a lot (of), much, many	87
Present tense with certain time expressions	88
Modal verbs in present perfect tense	89
Mixed tenses (present simple, present progressive, going to-future, will-future, past tense simple, past tense progressive, present perfect tense)	90
Words	92
Key	95

FILL IN REGULAR AND IRREGULAR PAST FORMS

go	....	hurt	....	bring	....
teach	....	write	....	feel	....
make	....	give	....	catch	....
call	....	bite	....	cross	....
think	....	buy	....	run	....
meet	....	play	....	spend	....
cut	....	throw	....	dig	....
lose	....	send	....	come	....
forget	....	jump	....	stay	....
put	....	shut	....	say	....
take	....	read	....	do	....
set	....	sing	....	pay	....
have	....	blow	....	begin	....
visit	....	arrest	....	bark	....
watch	....	hop	....	see	....
speak	....	swim	....	plan	....
marry	....	stop	....	study	....
choose	....	arrive	....	find	....
drive	....	hear	....	break	....
build	....	draw	....	drink	....
die	....	hurry	....	enjoy	....
stink	....	feed	....	hold	....
know	....	let	....	open	....
ring	....	work	....	try	....
steal	....	knock	....	sleep	....
eat	....	get	....	grow	....
hide	....	hit	....	shake	....
sell	....	shine	....	laugh	....
shoot	....	win	....	wear	....
weep	....	tell	....	stand	....
wake	....	leave	....	fall	....
want	....	greet	....	can	....
must	....	be	....	turn	....
fly	....	become	....	cost	....
fight	....	freeze	....	lend	....
hang	....	keep	....	lay	....
show	....	sink	....	spring	....
strike	....	tear	....	flee	....

PUT INTO PAST TENSE, NEGATE AND FORM QUESTIONS

1. I always tell my friends about school.
2. He can come at four.
3. I make a birthday cake in the evening.
4. We always play tennis after six.
5. She pays for our dinner at the restaurant.
6. The children are good at skiing.
7. We buy some nice computer games.
8. She tries to catch Bill.
9. The children make masks at school.
10. I hope to get some nice presents.
11. They pack their suitcases.
12. They act out stories at school.
13. We know a lot about this town.
14. They go for a walk on Sundays.
15. We cut out paper butterflies.
16. He puts his arm round her shoulders.
17. I want blue trousers.
18. We write a lot of letters to our pen friends.
19. Ann brings the flowers to her mum.
20. Peter takes the poster off the wall.
21. In our holidays we have breakfast at nine.
22. She cooks for us.
23. We eat meat every day.
24. There's a snake in the grass.
25. We read a lot of good books.
26. He always does his homework after school.
27. We need new trousers.
28. We look at the pictures.
29. He often buys sweets for Tom.
30. I have a party on my birthday.
31. We go to see our granny.
32. He runs home to have lunch.
33. He meets her in the evening.
34. He lays the book on the table.
35. We must hurry.
36. Peter pays the bill.
37. We know them well.

38. She hides in the locker.
39. He cuts his finger.
40. He hears her.
41. She says "Hello".
42. Mother sings a song.
43. The children run home.
44. We swim in the lake.
45. He sits on a chair.
46. He tells her everything.
47. We spend a nice holiday.
48. Peter eats a lot of ice cream.
49. Frank gives him the beer bottle.
50. Sandy can find his keys.
51. The plane leaves at six.
52. He gets a parcel from his uncle.
53. Susan wants a lolly.
54. Alice takes the hamburger.
55. Her hair is black.
56. Ann stays with her aunt.
57. My pullover is from Paris.
58. Sue reads a thrilling book.
59. Pit runs to the bus because he is late.
60. We visit our granny in the holidays.
61. The new hat is five pounds.
62. He gets a letter from Sally.
63. He offers her a cup of coffee.
64. Tom goes to market to buy eggs.
65. Bob takes Mandy to town.
66. The Smiths come early in the morning.
67. Sarah likes Frank.
68. The children go to the football match.
69. She looks pale.
70. The ambulance takes him to hospital.
71. Bob is very tired.
72. Phil stays in Vienna with his best friend.
73. The weather is terrible.
74. The Millers go to Italy.
75. He always thinks of Mary.
76. Our teacher gives us a lot of homework.
77. Our neighbours go by plane.
78. She writes to Peter.
79. Bill spends his holiday in France.

DO YOU REMEMBER? – TENSES

1. Look, the cat .... (drink) a bowl of milk.
2. Mick .... (drink) a lot of beer yesterday.
3. Yesterday the children .... (play) chess.
4. Judy .... (visit) London next holidays.
5. Ann .... (prepare) dinner now.
6. We .... (meet) people from America two weeks ago.
7. Tom .... (like) books on animals very much.
8. My parents .... (be) in Spain last summer.
9. Sally .... (not / can) do her homework yesterday because it .... (be) so difficult.
10. The weather .... (be) wonderful last week.
11. The Millers .... (have) a party next Saturday.
12. Susan .... (must / do) her homework now.
13. In our last holidays we .... (go) swimming every day. We .... (have) lots of fun.
14. Susan always .... (bake) a cake for the weekend.
15. They .... (go) into the cave where the treasure .... (be) two weeks ago.
16. The cinema .... (be) between the baker and the sweetshop.
17. What .... (you / do)? – I .... (post) this letter for mum.
18. He .... (meet) his sweetheart tomorrow. That's why he .... (be) so happy. Look, he .... (jump) for joy!
19. We .... (knock) at the door but nobody .... (be) there yesterday.
20. The children .... (turn) around and .... (run) away very fast when they .... (see) the man last night.
21. We .... (must) help father in the garden yesterday afternoon.
22. I .... (must) hurry! She .... (wait) for me at the zoo.
23. Yesterday .... (be) an awful day for me: in the morning I .... (must) run to school because I .... (miss) the bus, then I .... (get) a bad mark in English and then I .... (lose) my purse.

ASKING AND EXPLAINING THE WAY

Translate:

1. Verzeihen Sie, ich suche die Post. Können Sie mir sagen, wo sie ist?
2. Können Sie mir helfen? Ich habe mich verirrt.
3. Ich bin ein Fremder, können Sie mir den Weg zur Oper sagen?
4. Ich bin Ausländer.
5. Ist das der richtige Weg zum Theater?
6. Bin ich am richtigen Weg zum Bahnhof?
7. Verzeihung, würden Sie so nett sein und mir den Weg zur Post erklären?
8. Ist die Post neben der Polizei?
9. Überqueren Sie den Platz und biegen Sie in die erste Straße links ein.
10. Gehen Sie um die Ecke und Sie werden den Bahnhof am Ende der Straße sehen.
11. Ich möche gerne etwas essen. Wo ist ein billiges Restaurant?
12. Gehen Sie geradeaus, biegen Sie rechts ab, und da ist ein Restaurant gerade gegenüber dem Bahnhof.
13. Wie lange werde ich zu Fuß zum Bahnhof brauchen?
14. Sie können das Kino nicht verfehlen. Es ist neben der Apotheke.
15. Sie müssen nach dem Kino links abbiegen. Das Spital ist gegenüber der großen Brücke.
16. Nehmen Sie lieber die zweite Straße rechts. Die Telefonzelle ist in der Parkstraße.
17. Wie lange wird der Bus zum Bahnhof brauchen?
18. Bin ich am richtigen Weg zum Touristeninformationsbüro?
19. Gehen Sie an der Brücke vorbei. Gehen Sie nicht hinüber. Biegen Sie bei der Ampel links in die Smithstraße ein.
20. Am Ende des Platzes werden Sie die Bushaltestelle sehen.
21. Sie können den Supermarkt nicht verfehlen. Gehen Sie geradeaus und biegen Sie bei der zweiten Straße links ab. Dann gehen Sie wieder geradeaus und biegen links ab.
22. Gehen Sie an der Polizei vorbei und biegen Sie nach dem Hotel in die dritte Straße links ein. Sie können den Zoo nicht verfehlen.
23. Ich werde den nächsten Passanten fragen, wo ein Bäcker ist.
24. Biegen Sie in die kleine Straße links ein und Sie stehen vor der Kirche.
25. Darf ich Sie um den Weg zur Oper fragen?
26. Gehen Sie die Straße hinunter und warten Sie bei der Bushaltestelle.
27. Bin ich auf dem richtigen Weg zum Krankenhaus?

MODAL VERBS

CAN   to be able to   können, fähig sein

Present tense:	I **can** help you.	I'**m able to** help you.
	We **can** come.	We **are able to** come.
	I **cannot** see him.	I'**m not able to** see him.
		I'**m unable to** see him.
		(to be unable to = unfähig sein)
Past tense:	I **could** hear him.	I **was able to** hear him.
	I **could not**, I **couldn't**	I **was not able to**
		I **was unable to**
Future:		I **will be able to**
		I **won't be able to**
		I'**ll be unable to**

MAY   to be allowed to   dürfen

Present tense:	I **may** go to the party.	I **am allowed to** go to the party.
	We **may** visit Peter.	We **are allowed to** visit Peter.
Past tense:		I **was allowed to** meet him.
Future:		I **will be allowed to** go.

MUST NOT   not to be allowed to   nicht dürfen

Present tense: I **must not** watch TV.   I **am not allowed to** watch TV.

Past tense: I **was not allowed to** stay.

Future: I **won't be allowed to** play.

MUST   to have to / has to   müssen

Present tense: I **must** do my homework.   I **have to** do my homework.
                       She **must** help.   She **has to** help.

Past tense: He **had to** study.

Future: I **will have to** help.

DON'T HAVE TO = DON'T NEED TO = NEEDN'T =
= HAVEN'T GOT TO   nicht brauchen, nicht müssen

Present tense: I **don't have to** help him =
                       I **don't need to** help him =
                       I **haven't got to** help him =
                       I **needn't** help him.

Past tense: I **didn't have to** help him =
                       I **didn't need to** help him.

Future: I **won't have to** help him =
                       I **won't need to** help him.

MODAL VERBS

1. Mary .... (nicht müssen) come again tomorrow.
2. I .... (nicht brauchen) do my homework again.
3. Yesterday he .... (müssen) help his father in the garden.
4. We .... (dürfen) go to Frank's party last week.
5. Next year I .... (nicht müssen / nicht brauchen) get up so early.
6. I .... (müssen) go now, but you .... (können) stay a bit longer, you .... (nicht müssen) leave now.
7. You .... (nicht brauchen) answer all the questions yesterday.
8. They .... (nicht müssen) read the whole book next week.
9. I .... (nicht dürfen) go to Frank's party because I had a bad mark in my test.
10. .... (you / dürfen) go to Paris next summer?
11. .... (you / dürfen) go to Paris last summer?
12. You .... (müssen) go now. It's late.
13. They .... (nicht können) swim, so they .... (müssen) stay at home.
14. .... (he / müssen) help his parents paint the fence tomorrow afternoon?
15. Since he had a bad mark in English he .... (nicht dürfen) visit Bill.
16. I .... (nicht brauchen) help her. She knows everything.
17. I hope I .... (dürfen) visit Mary this year.
18. You .... (nicht dürfen) watch late-night films.
19. I bet I .... (können) read this book in one week.
20. We .... (nicht müssen) wait for him. He was there.
21. I fear you .... (müssen) come again.
22. We were wet so we .... (müssen) change our shoes.
23. When .... (you / müssen) give the book back? – Next week.
24. When .... (you / müssen) give the book back last week? On Monday or on Tuesday?
25. Last week we .... (müssen) get up very early.
26. For our party next week I .... (müssen) prepare the sandwiches and Peter .... (müssen) look after the drinks, so you .... (nicht brauchen) do anything.

27. Our teacher always says that we ………………………… (müssen) answer in English and we ………………………… (nicht dürfen) talk during the lesson.
28. You ………………………… (nicht brauchen) water the flowers. I did it.
29. ………………………… (you / können) eat everything up yesterday? – No, I ………………………… (nicht können) and I ………………………… (nicht müssen).
30. I think I ………………………… (nicht müssen) go and see the doctor again. I feel fine.
31. You ………………………… (müssen) ring him up before tomorrow.
32. We ………………………… (müssen) wait till tomorrow.
33. You ………………………… (nicht dürfen) spend all your money on sweets.
34. I ………………………… (können) save a lot of money last year.
35. He ………………………… (können) pass all his exams last year.
36. Mother ………………………… (müssen) bake a cake for the weekend.
37. We ………………………… (müssen) change our clothes because it was too cold.
38. There is no bread left! We ………………………… (müssen) buy some for tomorrow.
39. Tom ………………………… (nicht dürfen) buy a second ice cream yesterday.
40. Fred missed the bus. He ………………………… (müssen) wait for the next one.
41. Laura ………………………… (nicht brauchen) take her pills any more.
42. Father ………………………… (nicht können) start his car yesterday.
43. You ………………………… (nicht dürfen) turn right at the corner.
44. Mary ………………………… (nicht können) drink her lemonade because she has a sore throat.
45. You ………………………… (nicht müssen) feed the birds in summer. They find enough food.
46. He ………………………… (nicht können) pay the bill tomorrow. He has no money.
47. She ………………………… (dürfen) go swimming next week.
48. Paul ………………………… (nicht brauchen) cut the grass because I did it.
49. I ………………………… (nicht können) catch a taxi, so I was late.
50. Visitors ………………………… (nicht dürfen) feed the animals.

51. I watered the flowers yesterday, so you .... (nicht müssen) water them.
52. He .... (nicht können) reach the vase, he was too small.
53. I .... (nicht brauchen) wake him up. He was awake.
54. I .... (können) do this exercise alone! I was so happy.
55. I .... (nicht brauchen) wait for more than ten minutes. Then he came.
56. You .... (müssen) take this medicine twice a day.
57. You .... (nicht brauchen) stay in bed if you feel better.
58. We .... (können) go outside because the weather was so fine.
59. My room is a mess. I .... (müssen) clean it tomorrow.
60. .... (you / können) do your homework? — No, it was so difficult.
61. I .... (nicht dürfen) see the horror film yesterday.
62. You .... (müssen) help me this afternoon.
63. .... (he / können) solve the riddle yesterday?
64. The doctor said that she .... (müssen) stay in bed.
65. On Austrian roads you .... (nicht dürfen) drive on the left.
66. It is late. Go to bed, you .... (nicht brauchen) study any longer.
67. Last month we .... (nicht können) go sledging because there was no snow.
68. After our holidays last summer, my brother .... (können) swim well.
69. I .... (nicht brauchen) wait because he was in time.
70. Sally .... (nicht dürfen) go to the cinema tomorrow.
71. I had no key so I .... (nicht können) open the door.
72. Last Sunday Sue .... (dürfen) wear her new dress.
73. She .... (nicht können) pass her driving test next week.
74. The children .... (nicht können) go to the zoo. They were ill.
75. Last Monday she .... (müssen) tidy her room.
76. We .... (nicht dürfen) swim in that dirty water.

77. She felt ill and .... (müssen) leave earlier.
78. You .... (nicht brauchen) ring the bell. I have the key.
79. They .... (nicht dürfen) smoke in her living room yesterday.
80. We .... (nicht müssen) drive fast, we had enough time.
81. You .... (nicht dürfen) drink this. It tastes awful.
82. The buses were full so I .... (müssen) take a taxi.
83. You .... (nicht brauchen) pick me up! I'll take a taxi.
84. I feel much better now. I think I .... (können) go to the concert tonight.
85. When she was in England she .... (können) understand nearly everything.
86. Sorry, I have no time. I .... (müssen) work this afternoon.
87. I told Peter he .... (nicht dürfen) go to Jim's party last Saturday.
88. You .... (nicht brauchen) look for a babysitter for tomorrow.
89. Frank .... (müssen) change his trousers because they were wet.
90. Sorry, I .... (nicht können) pick you up at the airport tomorrow.
91. Phil, you .... (nicht dürfen) say such nasty words!
92. My room was a mess so I .... (müssen) clean it.
93. I'm sure you .... (können) pass your exam next Friday.
94. You .... (nicht müssen) clean my shoes.
95. Mother was in a hurry. At first she .... (müssen) feed the baby, then she .... (müssen) go shopping.
96. Oliver, you .... (nicht dürfen) copy from Mary's testbook!
97. I am sure we .... (nicht können) do the homework till tomorrow. There's so much.
98. You .... (nicht müssen) cut the grass yesterday. Father did it.
99. I .... (können) help you in the garden tomorrow afternoon.
100. Sheila .... (nicht dürfen) stay at the party after midnight yesterday.

SHOULD / SHOULD NOT
OUGHT TO / OUGHTN'T TO

SOLLEN

You **should** tell your father about it.
Pit **should** forget what Tom said to him.
We **should** go home now.
She **should** tell him the truth.

NICHT SOLLEN

You **should not (shouldn't)** eat so many sweets.
You **should not (shouldn't)** tell him a lie.
You **should not (shouldn't)** forget her birthday.
You **should not (shouldn't)** come home too late.

EIGENTLICH SOLLEN

You **ought to** be at home by now. – I know, I **should**. / I know, I **ought to**.
 Du solltest jetzt eigentlich schon zu Hause sein.

You **ought to** finish your work. – You're right, I **should** / I **ought to**.
Du solltest deine Arbeit eigentlich beenden.

I **ought to** take my pills but I don't want to.
Eigentlich sollte ich meine Tabletten nehmen, aber ich mag nicht.

EIGENTLICH NICHT SOLLEN

You **oughtn't to** eat so much. – No, I **shouldn't**. / I **oughtn't to**.
You **oughtn't to** smoke so much. – I know, I **shouldn't**. / I **oughtn't to**.

WHAT ABOUT ...?   HOW ABOUT ...?

Wie wäre es mit ...?   Wie steht es mit ...?   Was ist mit ...?

What about my new jeans? Are they dry?
How about your brother? Is he better again?
I'd like a new T-shirt. — **How / What about** this one?
Let's hide! **What / How about** under the bed?
We need a second girl! **How about** Nancy?
How about a hamburger now? I'm hungry.
How about Uncle Bill? Has he written?

LIKE   WOULD LIKE   WANT   NEED

I LIKE: ich mag, ich habe gerne, mir gefällt

Do you like Ben?   *Magst du Ben?*
Do you like hamburgers?   *Magst du Hamburger?*
I don't like sweets.   *Ich mag Süßigkeiten nicht.*
Do you like Tracy's new car?

I WOULD LIKE: ich möchte gerne, ich hätte gerne, ich würde gerne

I would like (I'd like) to have a milkshake.
Mum, I'd like new trousers, please.
I would like to buy flowers for her.
I'd like to travel to Paris.

I WANT: ich will, ich brauche

I want a new pair of shoes.
I don't want to get up early in the morning.
Sally wants to leave early.
I don't want his help.

I NEED: ich brauche

What I need is a cold drink.
I need a new car.

TO OR TOO

TO **ist Präposition und gibt eine Richtung an: auf, hin, nach, zu**
Bill runs **to** school.
He must go **to** hospital.
The children go **to** Mary's party.
At nine the children go **to** bed.
Let's go **to** the cinema!
Pit goes over **to** Tim.
Mark came up **to** Mandy.

TO **bildet den dritten Fall:**
I'd like to talk **to** Ben.
She writes a letter **to** him.
Listen **to** me.
She gave the present **to** Linda.

TO **bildet den Infinitiv:** I'd like **to** leave now.
She wants **to** have a sandwich.
He hates **to** walk.
It's time **to** go.
He is going **to** spend his holidays in Greece.

TOO **= zu (sehr), betontes *zu*:** Your T-shirt is **too** small.
You are **too** young to see this film, Mary!
This car is **too** expensive for us.
The test wasn't **too** difficult for us.
This exercise is **too** easy for you.
It's **too** loud in here.
The soup is **too** salty.

TOO **= auch:**
He heard the noise, **too**.
She gave him a nice present, **too**.
Liz is tired, **too**.
Are you going to come to Rick's party, **too**?

TRANSLATION

1. Ich mag das blaue Kleid nicht. Wie wäre es mit dem grünen Kleid?
2. Verstecken wir uns! Wie wäre es mit dem Garten?
3. Ich brauche ein neues Heft.
4. Ich möchte gerne neue Jeans.
5. Frank will nicht nach Linz fahren.
6. Er will jetzt ins Bett gehen. Ich bin auch müde.
7. Ich habe eine neue Hose. – Was kostet sie?
8. Ich würde jetzt gerne einen Kaffee trinken.
9. Ich brauche keinen Babysitter!
10. Diese Hose ist zu lang.
11. Ich brauche ein neue Feder.
12. Gefällt dir mein Bild?
13. Sandy möchte gerne ein neues Spiel.
14. Ich will einen neuen Hut. Ich mag den alten Hut nicht mehr.
15. Sie will nicht spazieren gehen.
16. Kommt Peter auch? – Nein, er ist zu klein.
17. Ich möchte auch ein Stück Kuchen.
18. Wir spielen auch oft mit ihr.
19. Wie wäre es mit der grünen Hose? – Nein, sie ist zu lang.
20. Diese Übung ist zu leicht für uns.
21. Die Brille ist zu teuer.
22. Ich würde gerne kommen, aber wir fahren nach Wien.
23. Er mag nicht singen. Es ist ihm zu langweilig.
24. Meine Hose ist viel zu eng.
25. Ich möchte dir gerne helfen.
26. Ich möchte dich fragen, ob du kommen willst.
27. Wir gehen zum Park, um zu spielen.
28. Hör mir zu!
29. Ich möchte dir etwas sagen.
30. Ich will dir etwas sagen.
31. Ich muss dir etwas sagen.
32. Ich brauche eine Hilfe. Wie wäre es mit dir?
33. Backen wir einen Kuchen!
34. Möchtest du gerne mitspielen? – Ja, gerne!
35. Er will jetzt nach Hause gehen.
36. Er möchte jetzt nach Hause gehen.
37. Er will jetzt nicht nach Hause gehen.
38. Ich möchte ins Kino gehen.

39. Könnten Sie mir den Weg sagen?
40. Gehen wir in die Stadt!
41. Ich würde lieber zu Frank gehen.
42. Wie wäre es mit einer Pizza?
43. Diese Schere funktioniert nicht.
44. Würdest du mir bitte helfen?
45. Kommt! Helfen wir ihr!
46. Essen wir! Ich bin hungrig!
47. Ich sollte eigentlich jetzt bei Frank sein.
48. Du solltest nicht über sie lachen.
49. Was ist mit deinem neuen Zimmer?
50. Ich brauche zwei Sessel.
51. Vater will jetzt ins Bad gehen.
52. Ich möchte gerne eine Tasse Tee.
53. Schau mich an!
54. Du bist zu jung, um zur Party zu gehen.
55. Thomas braucht einen neuen Filzstift.
56. Möchtest du mit uns kommen?
57. Jenny will einen neuen Schirm.
58. Er möchte einen neuen Schreibtisch kaufen.
59. Der alte Tisch ist zu hoch.
60. Er möchte auch einen neuen Ford.
61. Du kannst die Jeans nicht tragen. Sie sind zu eng.
62. Ich möchte auch nach Paris fahren.
63. Sie versteckten Peters Schulsachen auch.
64. Ich hörte die Türklingel auch.
65. Plötzlich hörte er auch einen Lärm.
66. Könntest du mich in die Stadt bringen?
67. Würdest du gerne mit mir in die Stadt fahren?
68. Die Kinder brauchen Farbstifte.
69. Welche Farbe hat dein Kleid? – Es ist auch blau.
70. Die Tür war auch halb offen.
71. Magst du Cornflakes?
72. Möchtest du jetzt Cornflakes?
73. Ich hasse Fleisch auch.
74. Gefällt dir das neue Buch von Thomas Brezina?
75. Wie wäre es mit einem Glas Milch?
76. Er ging auch nach Hause.
77. Susanne braucht auch eine neue Schultasche.
78. Sie konnte ihren Augen nicht trauen: Tim wollte Mary küssen!
79. Er konnte nicht kommen.

DURING   WHILE   (während)

DURING + NOUN (Hauptwort)
WHILE + VERB (Zeitwort)

1. I went to sleep .... the film because it wasn't interesting.
2. Brian wrote many cards .... his holidays.
3. We didn't talk .... dinner.
4. .... we are playing she is sleeping.
5. I was not nervous .... the exam.
6. We left .... the film because it was too boring.
7. She learnt a lot .... her stay in England.
8. He was in Russia .... the Second World War.
9. The window broke .... the storm.
10. .... we are waiting for him we are listening to the radio.
11. He made a call .... you were not at home.
12. Sally writes many letters .... she is on holiday.
13. It was funny .... the lesson.
14. I am reading the newspaper .... I am waiting for him.
15. Don't eat .... the lesson, please.
16. We had no water .... the day today. They turned it off.
17. Mrs Fisher waters my flowers .... my absence.
18. He fell asleep .... the lesson.
19. .... his studies in England he met Linda.
20. My mother can knit .... she is reading the newspaper.
21. We visited Paris .... our holidays.
22. They are singing songs .... they are walking.
23. They sang songs .... their hiking tour.
24. I can't do my homework .... the film.
25. I am ironing .... I am watching TV.
26. We often go for a walk .... the week.
27. Be quiet .... the lesson, please.
28. .... she is eating she is chatting.
29. She was sick .... the party.
30. She fell asleep .... the concert.
31. Tommy always cries .... I am on the telephone.
32. Granny cannot sleep well .... the night.
33. It rained a lot .... the night.

SOME

1) We use **some** in **positive** sentences.

Compounds
(Zusammensetzungen)

somebody	jemand
someone	jemand
something	etwas
somewhere	irgendwo
somehow	irgendwie

Ann bought **some** new shoes.
Somebody stole my bike.
There's **someone** at the door.
I can see **something** over there.
I found the shell **somewhere** on the beach.
We can do it **somehow**.

2) We use **some** in **questions where we expect the answer "yes"**.
(z.B. bei höflichen Fragen, wenn ich jemandem etwas anbiete)

Would you like **some** more tea? — **Yes,** please!
Can I have **some** of these apples? — **Yes,** of course!
Would you like **something** to eat? — **Yes,** please!

ANY

1) We use **any** in **negative** sentences.

   Compounds
   anybody
   anyone
   anything
   anywhere
   anyhow

   They have**n't** got **any** children.
   I do**n't** like **any** tomatoes.
   I can**not** see **anybody**. It's too dark.
   She **refused** to say **anything**. (sich weigern ⇨ negativ)
   He **never** does **any** work.
   He left home **without any** money. (ohne ⇨ negativ)
   I could**n't** find him **anywhere**.
   He could **hardly** say **anything**. (hardly = kaum ⇨ negativ)
   He has **hardly any** money left. (Er hat **kaum** Geld übrig. ⇨ **negativ**)

2) We use **any** in **questions where we expect the answer "no"**.

   Have **any** of you seen Tom? — **No**, we haven't.
   Is **anyone** there?

3) We use **any** in sentences with **if** (wenn, falls).

   If anybody has a question, please ask.
   If you need **anything**, just ask for it.
   Buy some apples **if** you see **any**.
   If any letters arrive for me, put them on the table.

4) We use it in **positive sentences** to express „**jeder beliebige, was (immer) du möchtest**":

   You can have **anything you want**!
   Take **any** cake **you like**!

SOME ANY AND COMPOUNDS

1. She bought .... new trousers.
2. I've got .... in my eye. It is red.
3. They haven't got .... boys in their class.
4. He's a lazybone. He never does .... homework.
5. Mother left home without .... money, so she couldn't buy ....
6. He refused to tell .... about his holidays.
7. If .... has got .... questions, I'll answer them.
8. If you need .... , just ask your teacher.
9. Have you got .... money? – No, I forgot my purse.
10. Did .... see Tom at the party yesterday? – No, I don't think he was there.
11. What's wrong with your left eye? – I have got .... in it.
12. Would you like .... more tea? – Yes, please.
13. Can I have .... of these toffees? – Yes, just help yourself!
14. I must have .... in my shoe. Perhaps there's a little stone ....
15. My key must be .... I saw it a few minutes ago.
16. You can take .... bus. They all go to Linz.
17. You can come and see me .... time. Whenever you want to.
18. Which sandwich should I take? – .... ! They are all super!
19. You can have .... present you want for your birthday.
20. Which song should I sing? – .... They are all beautiful.
21. There's .... at the door for you. He wants to ask .... questions.
22. Is .... there? I can hear ....
23. If .... wants to leave for the bus now, he can go.
24. Oh no! .... stepped on my glasses!
25. .... broke our neighbour's window.
26. The boy refused to tell us ....
27. Does .... mind if I smoke in the living room?
28. Would you like .... to eat now?
29. Do you live .... near the Bakers? – Yes, just opposite.
30. She wants to slim. She refuses to eat ....
31. .... rang the bell. Can you have a look?
32. When we were on interrail tour we didn't have .... money for a hotel, so we slept .... in the park.
33. Can I have .... lemon juice in my tea, please?

34. What are you looking for? – My left shoe must be .... under my bed!
35. There's .... green in my milk! – Come on, drink it! I can't see ....
36. You can have .... of my stamps. I don't need all of them.
37. The film is great. You can ask .... you like.
38. Can you give me .... information, please?
39. With this tourist pass you can go .... you like.
40. If .... asks you .... , don't tell him .... It is a secret!
41. If .... saw the accident, contact the police, please.
42. You can tell him .... you like. He doesn't tell ....
43. You may come .... day you want.
44. You can phone .... time you like. – I should be .... in the house.
45. Nobody tells me ....
46. She didn't tell .... about her plans.
47. I can't find my ring .... But it must be ....
48. I'm going to buy .... eggs.
49. I'm not going to get .... meat.
50. There isn't .... ice in the fridge. Please go and get ....
51. The children didn't make .... mistakes in the last exercise.
52. I can't find my brother .... , but I know he is hiding ....
53. Would you like .... tea now? Or would you like .... beer?
54. Can I have .... grapes, please?
55. Can you lend me .... money? – Sorry, I can't lend you .... money. I'm broke.
56. Would you like .... more soup?
57. I'm making .... coffee. Would you like .... ?
58. I ate .... hamburgers, but I didn't like them.
59. I can pay for you. I've got .... money with me.
60. There aren't .... trees in this town.
61. They don't have .... children.
62. Have you got .... brothers or sisters? – Yes. I've got two brothers.
63. You have got .... nice rings.
64. I don't hear .... They can't be in.
65. But .... must be at home!
66. Are there .... birthday cards for me this morning?

67. I need .... to drink. But there isn't .... restaurant ....
68. I haven't got .... stamps, but Jill has got ....
69. I must find .... for his birthday.
70. I'm thirsty. Can I have .... tea, please?
71. Don't buy .... bread. There's still .... left.
72. We visited .... very interesting places when we were in Rome.
73. .... to drink? – Yes, please.
74. Sheila wants to wash her hair. Is there .... shampoo left for her?
75. I'm going to the supermarket to get .... meat.
76. We had .... problems with the car. It didn't want to start.
77. There aren't .... sausages in the fridge. Go and buy .... , please. – What kind of sausages? – .... !
78. Do you need .... to write on? – No, thanks, I've got .... paper.
79. She said .... to me but I didn't understand. It was too loud.
80. I won't eat .... now, I had .... soup an hour ago.
81. There isn't .... in the fridge. It's empty.
82. I don't need ....
83. Can you lend me .... books?
84. Do you know .... about your home town? – Yes, I know .... important facts.
85. He doesn't speak .... foreign languages.
86. .... friends couldn't come to Linda's party.
87. I haven't got .... to put on. I must buy .... new.
88. We are going to spend our holidays .... in Greece.
89. Should I go and get .... water for you?
90. Would you like .... cold to drink? – Yes, please .... lemon juice with ice.
91. I can feel .... soft in the box.
92. He lives .... in the north of the city.
93. Give me .... more time, please.
94. There's .... in my hair! Look if it is a spider!
95. I couldn't get .... tickets for the theatre.
96. But I got .... tickets for the concert tomorrow.
97. I said, "I'll take .... ticket that is left!"
98. .... stole her scarf in the restaurant.
99. Could I have .... lemonade, please? – I'm so sorry, but there isn't .... left!

100. She ran away without saying .... She was hurt.
101. I can't do .... before he comes home.
102. Please look everywhere! The ring must be .... !
103. .... more cake? – Yes, please!
104. There isn't .... Coke left. Can you get .... from the supermarket?
105. I didn't meet .... last night. It was boring.
106. You can call me .... day you like, at .... time!
107. .... pupils think they will get a good mark without studying ....
108. She came in without saying "Hello" to ....
109. If you meet .... tell him that I'm .... in the garden.
110. What kind of music do you like? – ....
111. Can I have .... butter on my bread?
112. He refused to tell .... about the accident.
113. That's not true! .... crashed into my car!
114. I know the children are hiding .... , but I can't see them ....
115. If there's .... milk left, I'll have a glass.
116. Do they live .... near the Millers?
117. There is .... on the phone for you.
118. Can you give me .... advice, please?
119. .... forgot his umbrella in the umbrella-stand.
120. I hope you've got .... money with you, because I haven't got ....
121. Which bus will take me to town, number nine, ten or eleven? – .... of them!
122. Does .... mind if I go now? Does .... still need me?
123. You can take .... stickers. I don't collect any more.
124. Which book shall I read? – .... They are all interesting.
125. Can I do .... for you?
126. Do you need .... help?
127. She couldn't tell me .... interesting.
128. He refused to give us .... money. So we went away without .... money.
129. Goodness me! .... sat on my new hat!
130. If there is .... Coke left, put it into the fridge.
131. He did not want to tell me .... about his problems.
132. You don't make .... mistakes any more, am I right?

ONE   ONES

Man benötigt *one* und *ones*, um Wortwiederholungen zu vermeiden.

One ersetzt ein Hauptwort in der Einzahl.
Ones ersetzt ein Hauptwort in der Mehrzahl.

Merke: the little ones = die Kleinen, die Kinder
the little one   = der / die Kleine, das Kind

Achtung: one, ones stehen (meist) **NICHT** ⇨

⇨ 1. **nach unzählbaren Stoffnamen** wie: tea, coffee, wine, beer, milk, lemonade ..., wenn über sie eine **allgemeine Aussage** gemacht wird und sie **ohne Artikel stehen**.

  a) I prefer cold water to warm. (**kein** Stützwort **one**)

  b) I'll take **a** pink lemonade now, or should I take **a** red **one**?
  (mit Stützwort, da es sich um eine **spezielle Situation** handelt und **der Artikel** steht).

⇨ 2. **nach "own"**
This is a book I've just borrowed (*das ich mir gerade ausgeborgt habe*), but that book is my **own**.
This is my brother's bike and the red one is my **own**.

⇨ 3. **unmittelbar nach Zahlen**
Ben has got sixty Brezina books! I've only got **twenty**.
If you like my stickers you can have **three** or **four**.

⇨ 4. **wenn nach that/those "of" folgt**
The trees in our garden are smaller than **those of** Aunt Mary.
Julian's sister is nicer than **that of** Peter.
Mandy's cap is cooler than **that of** Frank.

⇨ 5. **nach dem Genitiv (2. Fall)**
This is Paula's pen, and this is **Nick's**.
My felt-tip is blue and **Julia's** is red.

1. Sam has got a blue school bag. I have got a green ....
2. I don't like this coat. Can you show me a smaller ....
3. I prefer Austrian tomatoes to Spanish ....
4. I'll take these red flowers and those yellow ....
5. Tommy has got wooden cars and metal ....
6. Tim and Sue! The little .... go to bed now!
7. Do you prefer black coffee or white .... ?
8. I like white wine better than red ....
9. Our garden is bigger than that .... of our neighbour.
10. I'll take the white mouse. Which .... do you like best? – The black ....
11. Sally's mascot is a blue magic stone. My mascot is a green ....
12. I have got a big doll and two small ....
13. She has got four dolls. I've only got two ....
14. Have you got a mountain bike? – No, just a normal ....
15. I am afraid of big dogs but I love small ....
16. I prefer the sandwiches with tomatoes. – Which .... ? – I said, "with tomatoes".
17. My best friend is Charles, and Tony's .... is Bill.
18. Fred has got sixty stickers. I've only got forty ....
19. Our car is dark blue, that .... of our neighbour is green.
20. What should I take now? A red wine or a white .... ?
21. I normally drink light beer, not strong ....
22. These are the children's bikes. That is my own ....
23. Which trousers do you prefer? The tight .... or the wide .... ?
24. My friend has got six hundred different stamps. I've only got two hundred ....
25. I'm going to get some red apples and some green ....
26. Which car is your car? This .... or that .... ?
27. His glass is greasy. He is asking for a new ....
28. Don't take this hat. The other .... is much better.
29. In the first box there are six white mice. In the second there are eight ....
30. Which hotel does Mr Miller stay at? – The .... opposite the park.
31. Your pancake was tasty. I'll have another .... , please.
32. Which keys are your keys? – The .... over there on the table.
33. Harry's specs are cooler than those .... of Pit.
34. This is Simon's book, and that is Ben's ....
35. Have you got a present for the little .... ?
36. This is my brother's room and that is my sister's ....

EVERY   EACH   ALL

EVERY **jeder** aus einer **großen, unbestimmten Gruppe**

Nach *every* steht das **Verb im Singular**.

Examples: Nearly every girl likes dolls.
I listened to every word he said.

Compounds:

everybody	jedermann
everyone	jedermann
everything	alles
everywhere	überall

Important expressions:

every time	jedesmal
every other day	jeder / jeden 2. Tag
every three hours	alle 3 Stunden
every now and then	von Zeit zu Zeit
everyday clothes	Alltagsgewand
everyday shoes	Schuhe für den Alltag
everything that	alles was
every morning	jeder / jeden Morgen
every day	täglich, jeder / jeden Tag
every year	jedes Jahr
every weekend	jedes Wochenende

EVERY   EACH   ALL

EACH   jeder (Einzelne) aus einer **bestimmten, kleineren Gruppe**

Nach *each* steht das **Verb im Singular**.

Example: Each student of St. Quentin High School got a medal.

Important expressions:

each of us	jeder von uns
each person **here**	jeder hier
They are 5p **each**.	Jedes / Jeder Einzelne kostet 5p.
They love **each other**.	Sie lieben einander.

ALL   **ALL + noun in singular**   ganz
          ALL + noun in plural   alle

Important expressions:

all day	der ganze / den ganzen Tag
all night	die ganze Nacht
all evening	der ganze / den ganzen Abend
all at once	ganz plötzlich
all of a sudden	ganz plötzlich
not at all	überhaupt nicht
no money at all	überhaupt kein Geld
no time at all	überhaupt keine Zeit
all that	alles was
first of all	zuerst, zu allererst, zunächst einmal
all the time	die ganze Zeit
All the best!	Alles Gute!
all my friends =	
all of my friends	alle meine Freunde
all _of_ **us**	wir alle
all _of_ **them**	sie alle

EVERY   EACH   ALL

1. .... family in our town has got a car.
2. The boys were playing in the garden. .... was very dirty.
3. They come to us .... weekend during the holidays.
4. .... day I must go to school by bus.
5. We have got English on .... of these days: Tuesday, Wednesday and Friday.
6. Nearly .... child likes strawberries.
7. .... of a sudden he went blue in the face.
8. Do .... of you speak English well?
9. There are three windows on .... side of their house.
10. .... teenager likes to go to the disco.
11. .... boy likes to ride his bike.
12. .... of these girls here is a model.
13. .... dog likes meat.
14. .... dogs dislike cats.
15. I enjoyed .... minute of the film.
16. .... of these people here is a winner.
17. He has got three brothers. They are .... very clever.
18. .... flower must be watered.
19. .... flowers must be watered.
20. She likes .... her classmates.
21. .... trees lose their leaves.
22. She had a bottle in .... hand.
23. She loves her two cats. .... cat gets a bowl of milk in the morning.
24. .... day we have breakfast at seven.
25. .... of us had a nice holiday.
26. .... monkeys like bananas.
27. Grill the fish for five minutes on .... side.
28. Is .... of you ready?
29. She must take a pill .... three hours.
30. He pays a visit to me .... now and then.
31. .... member of our team has a red ribbon.
32. .... the boys love football.
33. He comes to see me .... day.
34. The headmaster visited our class and asked .... child a question.
35. .... the people who know her like her.
36. .... of them knew the answer.

37. .... that he said was true.
38. The tourists entered the hotel. .... was carrying a heavy suitcase.
39. .... man must do his best.
40. She visited her mother in the hospital .... day.
41. The explosion broke .... the windows in the street.
42. The tickets are 20 pounds ....
43. She has got a new dress for .... day of the week.
44. Some children do not like watching TV at ....
45. He spends .... his money on sweets.
46. You can find Coke in .... part of the world.
47. .... of us liked the film.
48. We went to the museum .... other day.
49. I must feed my hamster .... day.
50. Nearly .... schoolchild knows that.
51. .... Austrian children can ski.
52. .... likes Linda because she is so sweet.
53. I want to grow my hair. .... girl in my class has got long hair.
54. In summer nearly .... is at the seaside.
55. .... year the Millers go to Carinthia.
56. I told Ben ....
57. First of .... you must look for your ring ....
58. .... likes flowers.
59. His name is Alexander but .... calls him Sandy.
60. I think .... can do this exercise alone.
61. .... time I meet him we have a wonderful evening.
62. We visit Uncle Mark .... four weeks.
63. .... I said to her was true.
64. .... time I see Fred he tells me a stupid joke.
65. Mother gave .... of us a glass of milk.
66. .... of the boys said it was true.
67. .... applauded after the concert.
68. There are trees on .... side of the road.
69. .... country has got a national anthem.
70. Yesterday it was cold .... day.
71. He gets the newspaper .... day.
72. How often do you watch TV? — .... evening.
73. .... the houses in this street look the same.
74. We spend our holidays in Turkey .... summer.
75. Mother has to work .... day.
76. .... of us needs a good friend.
77. Frank has got .... he needs: a nice wife and healthy children.

78. I must stay in bed .... day. I've got the flu.
79. .... is very friendly in our school.
80. He fell down .... at once.
81. .... the people were present.
82. .... zoo has got lions and bears.
83. .... children must go to school till fifteen.
84. Let's .... meet at the corner of King's Street.
85. .... boy and girl in 2A is clever.
86. .... of us has got a TV set at home.
87. .... of the zoos has wild animals.
88. .... children like ice cream.
89. .... of the children over there is from 4B.
90. Do .... of you like comics?
91. .... child wants to have toys.
92. .... girls in our class are nice.
93. Nearly .... children like animals.
94. Let's sing and play .... together.
95. .... elephant in the circus can dance.
96. .... of these parrots here can speak.
97. .... of us are hungry now.
98. These peaches are 8p ....
99. The baby is hungry .... two hours.
100. I meet him .... now and then.
101. He went to the theatre in his .... clothes.
102. In our holidays we get up late .... morning.
103. .... shops in Carnaby Street are expensive.
104. He has to take a pill .... two hours.
105. .... of us had lots of cake for breakfast.
106. .... room in this hotel has got a balcony.
107. .... apple in this basket is tasty.
108. .... parents love their children.
109. .... of you must leave now. It is late.
110. The two brothers like .... other very much.
111. The boys play football .... afternoon.
112. Mother gives them 5 pounds .... for the funfair.
113. They had to stop for a rest .... ten miles.
114. He is looking for his purse .... , in .... corner, but he can't find it.
115. First of .... he showed me ....
116. .... of us has a car.
117. .... his friends help him.

AS OR WHEN

AS
1. als, während (Zeitstrecke)
2. da (ja), weil
3. wie, so wie
4. as if – als ob
5. als, in der Rolle von
6. as for – was betrifft
7. as to – Höflichkeitsausdruck
8. the same as – der / die / dasselbe wie
9. as soon as – sobald als
10. as long as – solange
11. just as – gerade als
12. as well – genauso gut

WHEN
1. wann   (Zeitpunkt)
2. wenn, als
3. whenever – immer wenn

1. .... we are late we have to take a taxi now.
2. .... you come home you are going to have a nice meal.
3. He is not .... tall .... I am.
4. Tom Hanks plays .... Forrest Gump.
5. She is .... clever .... Pit.
6. .... will you come home? You sound .... if you've got a cold.
7. .... you are so cheeky, you'll get no pocket money.
8. I don't know .... he arrives.
9. The Millers are .... rich .... the Smiths.
10. .... do you normally have breakfast?
11. Since .... have you got a little brother?
12. She is getting nicer .... she gets older.
13. .... a child he was such a nice boy.
14. .... for you, you may leave.
15. Till .... can you stay?
16. Leave everything .... it is.

17. .... did that happen?
18. Tell me .... I can call.
19. I did .... he did and now I work .... a policeman.
20. .... were they at the airport?
21. Do .... you like!
22. You may go .... you are ready.
23. .... for me I must go now.
24. .... rich he is, I won't marry him.
25. He did a lot of climbing .... he was young.
26. Would you be so kind .... to close the window?
27. He is twice .... old .... I.
28. .... he was in France he learned a lot.
29. Madonna plays .... Evita Peron.
30. It was the same man .... yesterday. I remember exactly.
31. He did .... if I wasn't there.
32. You treat me .... a child.
33. Call .... you want to.
34. .... you yourself said, it is too late now.
35. It was raining .... we arrived.
36. .... do you want your tea?
37. Call me .... you are ready.
38. .... she is away I am sad.
39. He doesn't go out .... much .... you.
40. Bill is the same age .... I.
41. I can't work .... much .... she.
42. Tell me .... he comes.
43. .... the school year was over, she was happy.
44. .... you go away, please shut the windows!
45. .... I get up, I only have a cup of black coffee.
46. Sally hasn't got .... many friends .... I.
47. Sorry I couldn't come .... fast .... you.
48. .... the rain stops we are going to take a walk.
49. She is not .... old .... she looks.
50. Her hair has got the same colour .... her mother's.
51. I don't read .... much .... you do.
52. .... they live next to us, we meet once a week.
53. We came just .... Ben wanted to go.
54. Do .... father tells you.
55. I'd like the same drink .... yesterday.
56. You can take my car .... long .... you don't go too fast.
57. You may come at five .... well.
58. .... an Austrian I know how to prepare "Palatschinken".

COMPARISON OF ADJECTIVES

1. COMPARISON WITH -er, -est:

a) **one-syllable adjectives: (einsilbige, kurze Adjektive)**
Der **Mitlaut** nach einem **kurzen Vokal** wird **verdoppelt**.
Ein „y" nach Mitlaut wird in „i" verwandelt.
Ein „y" nach Vokal (a, e, i, o, u) bleibt erhalten.

big	bigger	biggest	*groß*
hot	hotter	hottest	*heiß*
glad	gladder	gladdest	*froh*
thin	thinner	thinnest	*dünn*
wet	wetter	wettest	*nass*
sad	sadder	saddest	*traurig*
fat	fatter	fattest	*dick*
nice	nicer	nicest	*nett*
dry	drier	driest	*trocken*
gay	gayer	gayest	*fröhlich*
small	smaller	smallest	*klein*
cold	colder	coldest	*kalt*

b) **adjectives with two syllables ending in: -er, -ow, -le, -y, -ly**
(Adjektive mit zwei Silben, die auf **-er, -ow, -le, -y, -ly** enden)
Stummes „e" vor der Endung -er, -est **entfällt**.

able	abler	ablest	*fähig*
noble	nobler	noblest	*vornehm*
gentle	gentler	gentlest	*sanft*
simple	simpler	simplest	*einfach*
clever	cleverer	cleverest	*klug*
tender	tenderer	tenderest	*zart*
narrow	narrower	narrowest	*eng*
shallow	shallower	shallowest	*seicht*

Ein „y" nach Mitlaut wird in „i" verwandelt.			
happy	happier	happiest	*glücklich*
pretty	prettier	prettiest	*hübsch*
easy	easier	easiest	*leicht*
holy	holier	holiest	*heilig*
lovely	lovelier	loveliest	*hübsch*

c) and following adjectives: Stummes „e" vor der Endung -er, -est **entfällt**.			
polite	politer	politest	*höflich*
quiet	quieter	quietest	*ruhig*
handsome	handsomer	handsomest	*fesch (boys)*
sincere	sincerer	sincerest	*ernst*
severe	severer	severest	*streng*
common	commoner	commonest	*häufig*
pleasant	pleasanter	pleasantest	*angenehm*
compact	compacter	compactest	*fest*
exact	exacter	exactest	*genau*
intense	intenser	intensest	*intensiv*
often (also see 2 b)	oftener	oftenest	*oft*

2. COMPARISON WITH *MORE* AND *MOST*:

a) adjectives with two syllables ending in -*ful* or -*re*:			
careful	more careful	most careful	*sorgfältig*
doubtful	more doubtful	most doubtful	*zweifelhaft*
useful	more useful	most useful	*nützlich*
awful	more awful	most awful	*schrecklich*
obscure	more obscure	most obscure	*unklar*

b) and following adjectives:

modern	*modern*	complete	*vollständig*
cautious	*vorsichtig*	correct	*richtig*
complex	*komplex*	corrupt	*korrupt*
content	*zufrieden*	wicked	*böse*
frequent	*häufig*	usual	*gewöhnlich*
perfect	*perfekt*	tired	*müde*
afraid	*Angst haben*	distant	*entfernt*
splendid	*hervorragend*	boring	*langweilig*
thrilling	*spannend*	often	*oft*

c) adjectives with three syllables or more:
Adjektive mit **drei und mehr** Silben:

interesting	*interessant*
beautiful	*schön*
characteristic	*charakteristisch*
frightening	*furchterregend*
exciting	*aufregend*
good-looking	*fesch*
intelligent	*intelligent*
comfortable	*bequem*

3. IRREGULAR COMPARISON:

good	better	best	*sorgfältig*
well	better	best	*gesund*
bad	worse	worst	
much / many	more	most	
little	less	least	*wenig*
little	smaller	smallest	*klein*

4. ADJECTIVES WITH TWO FORMS OF COMPARISON:

old	older	oldest
old	**elder**	**eldest**

elder / eldest: within a family o n l y **attributively** used.
(**nur** bei **Familienmitgliedern** und **nur beifügend** gebraucht
but: **älter als** = **older than**)

This boy is **older than** she is.
The theatre is **older than** the church.
It's the **oldest** building in town.

This is my **elder** brother.
He was his **eldest** son.
My **elder** sister is three years **older than** Liz.

far	farther	farthest	(*weiter* = örtlich)
far	**further**	**furthest**	(*weitere/s, noch welche/s, zusätzliche/s*)
			(ebenso für örtlich *weiter* zu verwenden)

Linz is **farther** from Vienna than Graz.
    (*weiter weg* = örtlich, der Entfernung nach)
This was his **farthest** journey.
    (*weiteste* = der Entfernung nach)

Can you tell me **further** news? (*weitere, noch welche*)
I'm going to buy **further** books. (*weitere, noch welche*)
I need some **further** information. (*zusätzliche*)
He took a **further** sandwich. (*noch eines*)
Any **further** questions?

| late | later | latest | (*später, neuest*) |
| late | la**tt**er | last | (*Letztere, Allerletzte*) |

See you **later**, Joe!
How about the **latest** news? (*neuesten*)
This is their **latest** hit. (*neuester*)
She knows everything about the **latest** fashion.

Mr Miller and Mr Perkins are teachers. The **latter** was
my teacher. (*der Letztere, Letztgenannte*)
Do you see Tim and Bill over there? The **latter** is my best friend.
The **last** news can be heard at midnight.
This was the **last** book he wrote, then he died.

| near | nearer | nearest | (*nächstgelegen*, räumlich) |
| near | —— | next | (*nächstfolgend*, Reihenfolge) |

The **nearest** hotel was closed, so I went to the **next**.
I missed the bus, so I had to wait for the **next**.
I must get off the bus at the **next** bus stop.
We are going to leave **next** week.

THAN

THAN is used after comparatives.
(wird nach der ersten Steigerungsstufe verwendet)

Tom is **older than** Bill.
It is **easier** to go by car **than** to go by train.
Gold is **more expensive than** silver.

> **ATTENTION:**
> We *say*: than me / than him / than her / than us / than them
>
> | **spoken** English (gesprochenes Englisch) | | **written** English (geschriebenes Englisch) |
> |---|---|---|
> | She is faster **than him**. | = | She is faster **than he is**. |
> | You are better **than me**. | = | You are better **than I am**. |
> | I was here earlier **than her**. | = | I was here earlier **than she was**. |
> | He is taller **than us**. | = | He is taller **than we are**. |
> | He was politer **than them**. | = | He was politer **than they were**. |

MORE   LESS

Did your coat cost 75 pounds? — No, **more than** that. (*mehr*)
The meeting was very short. **Less than** two hours. (*weniger*)
He eats **less than** I do (**than me**).

A BIT   MUCH   FAR   WAY

Sally is **much t**aller than Tom. (*viel größer*)
Peter is **far** better in English than I am. (*viel besser*)
Mary is only **a bit** younger than I am. (*ein bisschen jünger*)
She is **way** nicer than her sister. (*viel netter*) (gesprochen, informell)

AS ... AS
NOT AS ... AS
NOT SO ... AS

He is **as** friendly **as** she is. (*genauso ... wie*)
She is **as** old **as** I am. (*genauso ... wie*)
He is **not so** rich **as** they are. (*nicht so ... wie*)
She is **not as** nice **as** her sister. (*nicht so ... wie*)

THE SAME ... AS

My hair is **the same** colour **as** yours.
I arrived at **the same** time **as** Tom.
This pullover is **the same** size **as** her pullover.

MUCH   MANY

| much | more | most | *viel* | (unzählbar | + **Einzahl**) |
| many | more | most | *viele* | (zählbar | + **Mehrzahl**) |

much money *(see: p 87/3)*, fun, work, sleep ...
much milk, water, coffee, tea, juice, butter, cheese, jam ...

many problem**s**, coin**s**, house**s**, friend**s** ...
many people, children, men, women, fish, sheep ...
(see ☺I p 39 irregular plural)

LITTLE   FEW

| little | less | least | *wenig* | (unzählbar | + **Einzahl**) |
| few | fewer | fewest | *wenige* | (zählbar | + **Mehrzahl**) |

little   bread, time, sunshine, rain ...
few   ticket**s**, car**s**, animal**s**, sweet**s**, children, men, women, people ...

COMPARISON OF ADJECTIVES

1. The Millers have a .... (schnell) car. It's much .... than our car.
2. This newspaper is .... (interessant). It's the .... newspaper I know.
3. Mr Grant is a .... (gut) driver, but his wife is even ....
4. Susan is the .... (hübsch) girl in our class. — That's right. She is .... than all the others.
5. Tommy is a .... (nett) boy. He is .... than Fred.
6. There are .... (viele) parking spaces in our city and there will be many .... next year.
7. These apples are .... (teuer) than oranges. Last week they weren't as .... as oranges.
8. The food was .... (schlecht), but the drinks were even .... I won't go to that restaurant again.
9. This suitcase is .... (schwer) than all the others. Yes, it's the .... of them all.
10. The Coopers have the .... (schön) flowers in their garden. — No, I think your flowers are much .... than the Coopers'.
11. Is French as .... (schön) as English? — I think it's even .... than English.
12. Pullovers are .... (billig) in Austria than in France.
13. Hotels in England are .... (teuer) than in Italy.
14. A Skoda is not as .... (schnell) as a Mercedes.
15. A Rolls-Royce is .... (bequem) than a Ford.
16. My pullover was .... (billig) but Frank's was even .... than mine.
17. They live in a .... (groß) house, but Fred lives in a .... one.
18. I have got very .... (wenig) time. My mum has got even ....
19. She is a .... (klein) girl, but Susan is the .... of all.
20. Tim read .... (viele) books during the last holidays, Pit read .... and Tom read the ....
21. Pat has got .... (wenige) friends, but Sam has even got .... than Pat because he is a bully.

22. He is a .... (gut) doctor, you won't find a .... one.
23. This winter he caught a .... (schlimm) cold, even
    .... than last year.
24. My suitcase is .... (schwer) but Frank's suitcase is
    .... than mine. My parents' suitcase is the
    ....
25. This was a difficult test, much .... than last time. I think
    this was the .... test we have ever had (den wir
    je gehabt haben)!
26. My sister Helen is 10 years .... (jung) than I. She is my
    .... sister.
27. John is my .... (alt) brother. He's two years
    .... than I.
28. Mrs Smith is the .... (alt) woman I know.
29. Your photo is .... (gut) but my photo is
    .... than yours. But I must confess, Tim's picture is the
    ....
30. Yesterday the weather was .... (schlecht) but today it is even
    ....
31. Joe's handwriting is .... (schlecht) than Pat's but Sandy's
    is the ....
32. London is .... (weit) from here than Munich.
    New York is .... from here than London. It is the
    .... of these three cities.
33. If the .... (nächstgelegene) restaurant is closed, let's go to the
    ....
34. Where is the .... (nächste) bus stop?
35. The artist painted this picture one week before his death. It is his
    .... (letzte) picture.
36. Do you like the .... (neuest) song of the Scorpions?
37. This **is** the .... (neuest) **news**.
38. Good night, Ladies and Gentlemen. This **is** the .... (letzte)
    news of today.
39. Tom can jump .... (weit) than Bill but Sandy can jump
    .... of all.
40. Do you know the way to the .... (nächste) post office?
41. Mr Francis is a .... (fleißig) worker.
    He is .... than his friends.
42. Are there any .... (weitere) questions?

43. This is our .... (alt) daughter. She is two years .... than our son.
44. The .... (nächstgelegen) post office was closed so I ran to the ....
45. He always studies .... (wenig) time than we do but he reaches .... (gut) marks than we do.
46. Phil is .... (schlimm). He is the .... boy I know!
47. Simon is the .... (gut) pupil in class.
48. Normally he isn't very .... (sorgfältig), but today he was even .... than Susan.
49. Your homework is .... (schlecht) but Dan's work is even ....
50. John is very .... (dick). Tim is .... than he is but Frank is the .... of them all.
51. His work is .... (ordentlich), but her work is .... than his and my work is the .... of all.
52. Sally and Maggie are .... (gut) pupils. Sharon is the .... (klug) of them all.
53. Where is the .... (nächste) bus stop? — It's Wind Street.
54. When is there the .... (nächste) bus? — It's at midnight. This will be the .... (letzte).
55. Did you have any .... (weitere) homework? — No, that was all we had.
56. See you .... (später).
57. We missed the .... (letzte) bus.
58. Could you tell me where the .... (nächste) petrol station is, please?
59. Where will you spend your .... (nächste) holidays?
60. By road it is 2 miles to Dublin. By train it is .... (weit).
61. I met her at a party .... (letzte) night. She was the .... (letzte) to come.
62. It's .... (weit) to the supermarket than to the grocer's.
63. She has got .... (wenige) books than I have. But Tom has the .... of us.
64. Larry is well this year, much .... (gesund) than last year.
65. This film was the .... (interessant) film I've ever seen (den ich je gesehen habe).
66. His story is doubtful. But last time he told a story that was even much .... (zweifelhaft) than this one.
67. That's the .... (letzte) time I'll help you!

68. Where do you live? — It's easy to find. It's the .... (letzte) house in the road.
69. Shoes are .... (teuer) in Austria than in Italy.
70. Fred is .... (schwer) than the other children.
71. Tim is the .... (dünn) boy in our class.
72. Your composition is .... (schlecht) but Dick's is even ....
73. Oh, no! We missed the .... (letzte) train. We must take a taxi. It is much .... (teuer) than the train.
74. Phil is the .... (fesch) boy I've ever met (den ich je getroffen habe).
75. My sore throat is .... (schlecht) than yesterday.
76. Chris is the .... (gut) tennis player of our class.
77. I know you'll need no .... (weiter) help.
78. Today it is .... (windig) than yesterday.
79. He is the .... (böse) boy I've ever met (den ich je getroffen habe).
80. Mr Crisp is even .... (streng) than our last teacher.
81. Our trip this year was .... (angenehm) than last year. There were .... (weniger) tourists and there was .... (weniger) noise.
82. I hope this summer will be .... (trocken) than last summer.
83. This is the .... (groß) birthday cake I've ever got (den ich jemals bekommen habe)!
84. Last night's horror film was .... (spannend) than the week before.
85. I think horror films are .... (aufregend) than science fiction films.
86. You should eat .... (weniger) sweets, Ben.
87. Linda gets .... (wenig) pocket money than I do. But poor Frank gets the .... (wenig) of us three.
88. Belinda is the .... (schön) girl in town.
89. A football is .... (klein) than a basketball.
90. Paris is the .... (elegant) town I know.
91. Can you show me the way to the .... (nächste) phonebox?
92. You drink too .... (wenig). You must drink .... (mehr).
93. The flowers were .... (nicht so teuer wie) I expected.

AS ... AS,   NOT SO/AS ... AS,   THE SAME ... AS, MUCH,   A BIT,   FAR, THAN, LESS THAN, FEWER THAN, MORE THAN

1. Before tests Jill is .... (genauso nervös wie) Fred.
2. She is .... (schneller als) her elder brother.
3. The concert was .... (weniger als) an hour.
4. Brenda is .... (viel besser als) me.
5. Mrs Jones looks .... (viel jünger als) she is.
6. The tree is .... (ein bisschen höher als) our house.
7. My bike is .... (nicht so teuer wie) your mountain bike.
8. He called me at .... (derselben Zeit wie) yesterday.
9. Tim studied .... (weniger als) two days.
10. Your soup tastes .... (viel schärfer als) in Mexico.
11. Larry was .... (ein bisschen müder als) Linda.
12. The bus stop was .... (nicht so weit wie) I thought.
13. Sue's eyes are .... (dieselbe Farbe wie) her mother's.
14. He has got .... (viel mehr Zeit als) I have.
15. She has got .... (viel weniger Zeit als) last year.
16. They have got .... (viel weniger Abzeichen als) we have.
17. This work took me .... (weniger als) half an hour.
18. Today I'm .... (viel trauriger als) yesterday.
19. Our holidays were .... (nicht so teuer wie) I expected.
20. He earns .... (viel weniger als) last year.
21. He has got .... (viel weniger Marken als) I have.
22. We have got .... (dasselbe Auto wie) Uncle Bob.
23. Pit was .... (ein bisschen schlauer als) you.
24. The kids are .... (viel größer als) their English teacher.
25. She has got .... (viel weniger Probleme als) he has.
26. The test was .... (nicht so schwierig wie) I feared.
27. Your homework will take you .... (weniger als) twenty minutes.
28. Today's weather is .... (weniger angenehm als) yesterday's.
29. You make .... (viel weniger Fehler als) Tim.
30. Paul's party was .... (viel lustiger als) Patrick's.
31. Chinese is .... (genauso schwierig wie) Japanese.
32. Today Bob was .... (nicht so verwirrt wie) yesterday.
33. You drink .... (viel mehr Wein als) you can take (verträgst).

WILL-FUTURE

Forms: **I will = I'll**   **I will not = I won't**

WILL-FUTURE is used (wird verwendet):

A) If you are **not sure** or **expect, hope, fear** something.
(**Vermutungen, Erwartungen, Hoffnungen, Befürchtungen, unsichere Vorhersagen**)

B) It is used for **formal announcements (formelle Ankündigungen und Termine, offizielle Verlautbarungen, formelle Treffen, Sitzungen:** meetings, conferences, dates**)**

C) **Spontaneous decisions**
(spontane Entscheidungen im Moment des Sprechens: im Gasthaus, beim Essen, Trinken)

D) Wenn ein Ereignis **nur unter einer bestimmten Bedingung** stattfindet **nach** einem *if-Satz*

E) Wenn man **jemanden um etwas bittet**

Examples:

A) I <u>expect</u> they **will** be at home at ten. (Erwartung)
I <u>fear</u> we **will** be late. (Befürchtung)
She <u>hopes</u> she **will** have a nice time. (Hoffnung)
Do you <u>think</u> it **will** be hot tomorrow? (Vermutung, Vorhersage)
I <u>think</u> it **will** be warm and sunny. (Vermutung, unsichere Vorhersage)
I <u>bet</u> you **will** meet Frank. (Vorhersage)

B) The meeting of the Weight Watchers **will** be on Tuesday. (Termin)
The president **will** arrive at nine. (formelle Ankündigung)
The road **will** be closed in June. (offizielle Verlautbarung)

C) I'll take a hamburger and a Coke. (spontane Entscheidung)
Let me see, I'll have an ice cream cornet. (spontane Entscheidung)
I'm tired. I'll go to bed now. (spontaner Entschluss)

D) **If** it is so cold tomorrow, we **won't** go camping. (bestimmte Bedingung)
If you don't hurry, we**'ll** miss the train! (Bedingung)
If John is well again, we **will** go to Paris. (Bedingung)

E) **Will** you carry my suitcase, please? (Bitte)
Will you open the window, it's so hot? (Bitte)
Will you please stop smoking in the living room? (Bitte)

WILL-FUTURE is used with the following words and expressions:

expect	erwarten
fear	befürchten
hope	hoffen
worry	sich Sorgen machen
think	denken
probably	wahrscheinlich
perhaps	vielleicht
possibly	vielleicht, möglicherweise
maybe	vielleicht
It is possible that	Es ist möglich, dass
When I'm older ...	Wenn ich älter bin
When I'm seventeen	Wenn ich 17 bin
When I'm grown up	Wenn ich erwachsen bin
In twenty years' time	In 20 Jahren
bet	wetten
I'm afraid	ich befürchte
I'm worried	ich bin beunruhigt
promise	versprechen
wonder	gerne wissen wollen
doubt	bezweifeln
In that case	In diesem Fall

GOING TO-FUTURE

The **GOING TO-FUTURE** (**near future**) is used to express:

A) **Intention, plan** (persönliche Absicht, persönliche Pläne, Ferienpläne, Tagespläne etc.)

B) **Certainty** (persönliche Gewissheit)
I know
I'm sure of it (ich bin sicher)
I'm certain (ich bin sicher)

C) **Decision** (persönliche Entscheidung, aber kein spontaner Entschluss)

D) Something that is **quite sure to happen** (etwas, das ziemlich sicher eintritt: Wettervorhersagen.
Wenn es gewisse Anzeichen für das sichere Eintreffen der Handlung gibt.)

Examples:

A) I'm **going to** spend my holidays in Italy this year. (persönl. Plan)
I'm **going to** take the dog for a walk now. (persönl. Absicht)

B) I **know** that I'm **going to** be late. (persönl. Gewissheit)
I'm **going to** leave him. I'm **sure** of it. (persönl. Gewissheit)

C) Yesterday he told me about his problems and I'm **going to** help him.
(persönl. Entscheidung, nicht spontan getroffen)
I'm **going to** repair his car. It broke down yesterday.
(persönl. Entscheidung, nicht spontan getroffen)

D) It's **going to** rain. Look at the black clouds! (sichere Wettervorhersage)
Tom fell down. He is **going to** cry in a second. (sicheres Eintreffen einer Handlung)

WILL OR GOING TO

1. Are you worried that we .... miss the bus? — No, I think we .... be in time.
2. It .... snow. Look at the dark clouds.
3. She .... marry him.
4. I hope the weather .... be fine tomorrow.
5. I think he .... ask me a lot of questions.
6. She is worried that she .... be late for the meeting.
7. We expect that they .... arrive tomorrow.
8. What .... (you) do in your holidays?
9. Mother doubts that Linda .... get a good mark.
10. When I'm older I .... stay up very late.
11. I hope it .... (not) rain.
12. When she's eighteen she .... go to Salzburg to study there.
13. It .... probably snow next week.
14. What .... (you) do on Monday? — I think we .... visit granny.
15. The shop .... close at seven p.m.
16. I bet he .... (not) get a good mark, he's too lazy.
17. The winter holidays .... be in the third week in February.
18. I hope he .... (not) ask me about the broken window.
19. I don't think he .... be back in time.
20. I bet we .... have a boring weekend!
21. I know he .... help us.
22. She wonders what her friends .... do at night.
23. I'm sure that I .... meet him at six.
24. It is possible that they .... arrive on Friday morning.
25. I hope the teacher .... give us easier exams.
26. I .... take the blue pullover.
27. When I'm seventeen I .... have a nice friend.
28. There .... be a meeting at school for parents and teachers.
29. I bet he .... take you to the headmaster.
30. .... (you) stay out late?
31. I am afraid the dress .... be too tight. It .... (not) fit me.
32. There .... (not) be a meeting of the Dancing Club today.
33. When I'm older I .... go to a summer camp all alone.
34. I bet the meal in that restaurant .... be expensive.
35. .... (you) see the latest film with Kevin Costner?

36. I think I .... go to bed now. Perhaps I .... read a bit before I fall asleep.
37. On Saturday the Prime Minister .... be in London.
38. The black clouds are gone. It .... (not) rain.
39. The Camping Club .... organize a trip to France this year.
40. What .... (he) do after the final exam?
41. It is raining hard. Well, in that case I .... stay at home.
42. I .... have tea with my new friend.
    I think it .... be a nice afternoon.
43. The Wildlife Club .... meet at school at 8 p.m.
44. Do you want a pullover or a jacket? – I think I .... take the jacket.
45. Phil .... start judo lessons next week.
46. I hope there .... (not) be a thunderstorm while we are hiking.
47. What .... (you) take? – I think I .... take a hamburger and a Coke.
48. There .... (not) be a meeting of the Film Club today. It .... be on Friday instead.
49. I .... learn an instrument this year.
50. What would you like to drink? – I'................. have a cup of tea, please.
51. .... (you go) to the funfair? – No, I haven't enough money.
52. .... (she go) skiing? – No, she hurt her arm.
53. Something is wrong with my bike. Can you help me? – All right,
    I .... repair it for you.
54. Do you think your brother .... get the job?
55. This blouse is nice. But I am afraid it .... be too big.
    I .... try the green one.
56. The new tourists .... probably arrive at four o'clock.
57. He worked all night. He .... be tired today, I'm sure of it.
58. I hope Frank .... like the present you .... buy for him.
59. Did you fetch the medicine for me? – I completely forgot.
    But I .... fetch it now.
60. I expect that the weather .... be fine tomorrow.
61. Let's hope it .... (not) rain when we have our garden party.
62. My sister .... work on a farm in the summer holidays.
63. Mum buys some noodles because she .... prepare an Italian meal.
64. My dad .... get a new car next week.
65. In the summer holidays we .... travel through France.
66. We .... get a dog. – Oh no, it .... bite and make puddles on the carpets!
67. He .... probably not invite you.
68. This fur coat .... be expensive.
69. He .... learn Chinese. What a funny idea!

70. I bet he .... take you out to a snack bar and not to a restaurant.
71. I .... leave my blue dress on.
72. He was rather unfair to you. – Well, in that case I .... (not) help him.
73. They .... have a party. – That .... be great fun!
74. Dad .... take me to the opera!
75. I think I .... have a cup of coffee now.
76. .... (she / go) to the pop concert? – No, she hates pop music. I think she .... (not) go.
77. Do you hear the noise? Our car .... break down!
78. He didn't work hard. He .... (not) pass the exam.
79. The shops .... be closed on Sunday.
80. The planned trip to the Opera in Vienna .... (not) take place.
81. I promise I .... do my homework.
82. I think this exercise .... (not) be too difficult for me.
83. Do you want the cream cake or the fruit cake? – I .... take the fruit cake, please.
84. I'm afraid I .... (not) be able to come.
85. Which film do you want to see? The comedy or the horror film? – I think I .... see the comedy.
86. Our headmaster .... take part in a charity concert on Friday.
87. I bet you .... get married before me.
88. When I'm grown up I .... be a policeman.
89. I .... have some toast now, I'm hungry.
90. Where .... (you) spend your holidays this year?
91. In twenty years' time you .... have a lot of children.
92. We .... probably have a nice time this evening.
93. I think Diana .... have a good mark in her English test.
94. At this time tomorrow I .... probably be on the Eiffel Tower.
95. My bike is broken. Can you have a look at it, Danny? – Yes, Mary told me about it. I .... repair it in the afternoon.
96. I .... be at Tim's party this evening.
97. .... (you) be there, too?
98. Pit .... have a lot of exams this school year.
99. .... (you) please help me do my homework?
100. Of course, I .... help you.
101. .... (Bob) visit us this year?
102. I think I .... take a cheeseburger.
103. I .... write a letter to Aunt Maggie.
104. It .... snow. So put on your boots.
105. We hope the weather .... be fine at the weekend.
106. .... (she) write him again?

107. No, she ………………… (not) write him again.
108. There are dark clouds in the sky. There ………………… be a heavy thunderstorm.
109. Today I ………………… help father in the garden.
110. It ………………… be sunny tomorrow. There are no clouds in the sky.
111. We ………………… probably go to Greece next summer.
112. We ………………… spend our holidays in Greece.
113. Granny ………………… take a walk in the park.
114. They say it ………………… snow over Christmas.
115. What do you think the weather ………………… be like tomorrow?
116. You can leave your coat at home. It ………………… (not) be cold.
117. We ………………… probably go to Canada this summer.
118. What ………………… (you) do in your next holidays?
119. We ………………… spend our holidays in France as we do every year.
120. I think we ………………… spend our holidays in France.
121. Do you think Frank ………………… come to our party?
122. It is possible that he ………………… come tomorrow.
123. Mum is worried that Bill ………………… be late.
124. But I know he ………………… be in time.
125. I'm sure we ………………… have a fine time together.
126. The meeting of the Friends of Animals ………………… be on Tuesday.
127. Mum, I promise that I ………………… (not) be late!
128. Mary doubts that Peter ………………… win the first prize.
129. Phil wonders if Mary ………………… invite him.
130. I forgot to shut the window. I ………………… go and close it at once.
131. Do you think our team ………………… win the match?
132. If the weather is really cold and wet we ………………… stay at home.
133. ………………… (you) help me put the box on the locker?
134. Next year dad ………………… be forty. We ………………… have a big party.
135. Maybe she ………………… call me at eight. I ………………… stay at home and wait.
136. First I must do the washing-up, then iron the napkins, then feed the baby! — Cool down I ………………… do the washing-up for you!
137. Pit expects he ………………… get a letter from his girlfriend every day.
138. The football team ………………… arrive at the airport at ten.
139. The tunnel ………………… be closed from July to September.
140. If you don't run for your life they ………………… catch you.
141. ………………… (you) please stop shouting like mad?
142. I ………………… just have an apple, please.
143. I bet I ………………… (not) make any mistakes in my next test.

THE ADVERB

When must we use the adverb?
(Wann müssen wir das Adverb verwenden?)

> Das Adverb bestimmt, beschreibt ein **Verb** näher.
> Es zeigt, **wie** etwas getan wird.

Examples:

He writes **carefully**.	Er schreibt **sorgfältig**.
verb adverb	**Wie** schreibt er? – **Sorgfältig**.
	Adverb

She sings **beautifully**.	Sie singt **schön**.
verb adverb	**Wie** singt sie? – **Schön**.
	Adverb

Peter runs **quickly**.	Peter läuft **schnell**.
verb adverb	**Wie** läuft Peter? – **Schnell**.
	Adverb

It is snowing **heavily**.	Es schneit **heftig**.
verb adverb	**Wie** schneit es? – **Heftig**.
	Adverb

Beachte: Die **-ing form** ist ein **Verb**.

ATTENTION:

is, am, are, was, were, will be, have been, has been
sind **Hilfsverben** und haben ein **Adjektiv** nach sich.

Examples:
  She **is** *happy.*
  Lucy **was** *angry.*
  Linda **will be** *sad.*
  She **is** a *careful* girl.

Bildung des Adverbs:

1. durch Anhängen von -*ly*		
awful	— awful**ly**	*schrecklich*
careful	— careful**ly**	*sorgfältig*
final	— final**ly**	*endlich*
full	— ful**ly**	*völlig*
fantastic	— fantastic**ally**	*fantastisch*
careless	— caress**ly**	*schlampig*
honest	— honest**ly**	*ehrlich*
slow	— slow**ly**	*langsam*
loud	— loud**ly**	*laut*
quick	— quick**ly**	*schnell*
quiet	— quiet**ly**	*ruhig*
sad	— sad**ly**	*traurig*
beautiful	— beautiful**ly**	*schön*
true	— tru**ly**	*wirklich*
possible	— possi**bly**	*möglich(erweise)*
terrible	— terri**bly**	*schrecklich*
probable	— proba**bly**	*wahrscheinlich*
nice	— nic**e**ly	*nett*
extreme	— extrem**e**ly	*äußerst*
absolute	— absolut**e**ly	*völlig, absolut*
happy	— happ**i**ly	*glücklich*
easy	— eas**i**ly	*leicht*
angry	— angr**i**ly	*zornig*

2. Manche Adverbien haben dieselbe Form wie das Adjektiv			
early	—	early	*früh*
daily	—	daily	*täglich*
weekly	—	weekly	*wöchentlich*
monthly	—	monthly	*monatlich*
yearly	—	yearly	*jährlich*

3. Adverbs without *-ly*			
good	—	**well**	Mother cooks well.
long	—	**long**	Stay as long as you like.
fast	—	**fast**	Don't speak so fast.
straight	—	**straight**	Go straight ahead.
hard	—	**hard**	She works hard.
near	—	**near**	The dog comes near.
late	—	**late**	He came late in the evening.
fair	—	**fair**	Paul always plays fair.
high	—	**high**	The monkey can climb high.

ADJECTIVE OR ADVERB

1. Look out of the window. It is snowing .... (heavy).
2. I can do this test .... (easy).
3. Paul is very .... (clever).
4. He shouts .... (angry).
5. You write so .... (slow)!
6. This evening I am going to bed .... (early).
7. Mum opened the door .... (slow).
8. Mother came into the kids' room .... (quiet).
9. Tommy is sleeping .... (quiet).
10. Our homework is not .... (difficult).
11. Mother always speaks .... (clear) and .... (slow).
12. Our football team played .... (good).
13. She understands German .... (perfect).
14. Randy is really .... (perfect) at Maths.
15. Sue has got a .... (bad) cold.
16. Mick can run very .... (fast / quick).
17. We must be .... (quiet) and listen .... (careful).
18. Grandpa didn't sleep .... (good) last night.
19. Aunt Mary is a .... (good) cook. She cooks .... (good).
20. Simon is a .... (fair) and .... (good) football player.
21. Simon plays .... (fair) and .... (good).
22. These flowers are really .... (cheap).
23. Linda is .... (sad).
24. The guests dance .... (happy).
25. We get the newspaper .... (daily).
26. Come here .... (quick) and listen to me .... (careful).
27. Cliff is a .... (good) skier. He really skis .... (good).
28. Linda doesn't cook .... (good).
29. Mary sings .... (beautiful). She sings a .... (beautiful) song.
30. This little boy can run very .... (fast). He is a .... (good) athlete.
31. The teacher looked at her .... (angry).

32. Eric sings .... (bad).
33. Please write your composition .... (careful).
    It's not very .... (long) and you can do it
    .... (easy).
34. Sheila always answers .... (polite). She is a very
    .... (polite) girl.
35. Larry often behaves .... (bad) at school.
36. Please don't work so .... (careless).
37. Pit doesn't play .... (fair)!
38. Paul came .... (late) at night.
39. Don't go .... (near) this horse. It is
    .... (dangerous).
40. Lisa doesn't work .... (hard) enough for her test.
    She won't get a .... (good) mark.
41. Grandfather speaks Polish very .... (good).
42. We are always .... (busy) in the afternoon.
43. Shut the door .... (quick)!
    There is a .... (strong) wind.
44. Last week it rained .... (heavy). Now the pond is
    .... (full) of water.
45. Simon hurt his elbow .... (bad). He ran too
    .... (quick). He always runs far too .... (fast).
46. Are you .... (nervous) before an exam? – No, not at all,
    because I always study .... (careful).
47. Mum worked .... (busy) today, but now she is
    .... (tired) and goes to bed .... (quick).
48. Nelly always dresses .... (beautiful).
49. With this time machine you can look into the future
    .... (clear).
50. Don't press my arm so .... (hard)! It hurts
    .... (bad).
51. Mrs Grant is looking .... (happy) at her
    .... (lovely) flowers.
52. Barry shouted so .... (loud) that the baby couldn't sleep
    .... (good).
53. Mary draws very .... (good). She is a
    .... (good) painter.
54. The children are playing .... (happy) and they are singing
    .... (beautiful).
55. Robert can sing .... (fantastic).
56. The guests arrived .... (late).

57. We must go to bed .... (early) tonight because tomorrow we are going to climb a .... (high) mountain.
58. Susan plays the recorder .... (good). Her fingers dance up and down .... (quick).
59. Our kite flies .... (high) in the sky.
60. Run .... (quick) or you'll miss the bus!
61. Tim .... (proud) tells us that he is the winner of the first prize.
62. Sally .... (sad) went away.
63. She plays table tennis .... (good).
64. Mandy paints .... (wonderful).
65. That was a very .... (good) story and you told it .... (good).
66. The English lesson was fun, so it passed .... (quick).
67. The man in the lake .... (loud) shouted for help.
68. Linda .... (lucky) found her ring in the .... (high) grass.
69. Please cook .... (quick) because I'm so .... (hungry).
70. It was .... (cold) so we put on our coats .... (quick).
71. He was able to win the match .... (easy). He will be a .... (famous) player one day.
72. She .... (absolute) hates basketball.
73. He jumped .... (high) into the air.
74. Calm down and breathe in .... (deep).
75. You did your work .... (perfect).
76. The man went away .... (quiet) and .... (sad).
77. Nelly dresses .... (pretty).
78. Jimmy rode his bike too .... (fast) and fell down.
79. I must tell you .... (honest) that I don't like Jack.
80. Belinda smiles .... (nice).
81. They will .... (possible) come at nine.
82. Father reads the newspaper .... (daily).
83. Go .... (straight) ahead and turn left at the shop.
84. I'm going to pick you up .... (early) in the morning.
85. He sometimes drives .... (dangerous) and too .... (fast).
86. All monkeys can climb .... (high).
87. We pay the bill .... (monthly).
88. The speaker spoke too .... (quick) for us.

PREPOSITIONAL PHRASES

Manche Verben **ändern** ihren **Sinn**, wenn sie eine **Präposition** nach sich haben:

look	schauen
look **for**	suchen
look **after**	sich kümmern um
look **out**	aufpassen
look **into**	hineinsehen
look **back**	zurücksehen
look **down on**	verächtlich hinuntersehen auf
look **forward to**	sich freuen auf

Look! The man is climbing up the tree!
Peter must **look for** his key.
Linda **looks after** her little sister.
Look out! A car is coming!
Don't **look into** that box!
Don't **look back**, **look into** the future!
You mustn't **look down on** Peter just because he is younger!
We all **look forward to** the next holidays.

answer	antworten
answer **back**	zurückschnabeln

He must **answer** all the questions.
Don't **answer back**, you cheeky boy.

knock (**at**)	(an)klopfen
knock **over**	niederschlagen
knock **out**	k.o. schlagen

Simon **knocked at** the door.   Who **is knocking**?
The bully **knocked** the boy **over**.   The boxer **knocked** the man **out.**

watch	ansehen
watch **out**	aufpassen

Nelly **is watching** the film on TV.
Watch out! A car is coming!

leave	zurücklassen, verlassen
leave **alone**	in Ruhe lassen
leave **in** the lurch	im Stich lassen
leave **to** somebody	jemandem überlassen
leave **about**	herumliegen lassen
leave **out**	auslassen

He **left** his umbrella in the shop.
Don't **leave** your clothes on the ground.
He **left** her **in the lurch**.
Leave it **to** me, I'll do it for you.
Don't **leave** your things **about**! What a mess!
You **left out** nine words in this exercise!

break	brechen, ausbrechen (storm)
break **in / into**	einbrechen; jemanden unterbrechen
break **out**	ausbrechen (war, fire, violence)
break **down**	kaputt werden (car, machine)
break **off**	beenden
break **through**	einbrechen, durchbrechen

Don't **break** the vase, please!
Somebody **broke into** his house while he was away.
The ice isn't thick enough! You'll **break through**!
The sun **broke through** the clouds.
You always **break in** when I want to tell you something!
The old car **broke down**.
Stop your quarrel! **Break** it **off**!
He **broke off** in the middle of the sentence.

clean	reinigen
clean **out**	durchputzen, ausmisten
clean **up**	aufwischen, reinigen

Clean your teeth before you go to bed.
I must **clean out** the stable / attic.
There's water on the floor. **Clean** it **up**, please.

come	kommen
come **across**	zufällig treffen
come **on**	vorwärts, los
come **out**	herauskommen
come **round**	besuchen

He **came** at nine.
I **came across** him in town.
Come on! Let's hurry!
His lies **came out**.
His new book will **come out** in September.
Please **come round** for dinner.

give	geben
give **back**	zurückgeben
give **out**	austeilen
give **in**	nachgeben
give **up**	aufgeben

Give me a sandwich, please!
You must **give** the book **back** on Monday.
The teacher **gives out** the notebooks.
Give in, you know that I'm right!
He **gave up** smoking last year.
Never **give up** hope!

PREPOSITIONAL PHRASES

1. Sally can't find her lipstick. She is looking .... it everywhere.
2. Don't answer .... to your father! That's impolite!
3. I hear somebody knocking .... the door.
4. As I wanted to take the salt shaker, I knocked my glass ....
5. Hey! Watch .... ! You are spilling the milk on the table! Now you must clean it .... !
6. Father watches .... the news every evening.
7. Come ....! Leave me .... ! I have got to work.
8. Somebody broke .... Mr Simpson's house while he was away.
9. You always leave your things ....!
10. Dad gave .... smoking last year.
11. You always break .... when I am speaking!
12. Their new song will come .... in two months.
13. You have no chance! Give .... !
14. I came .... Nigel in town. He asked me to come .... next Friday.
15. I must go to the library. I have to give .... some books.
16. The burglar broke .... of prison.
17. I had to leave .... half of the exercises. They were too difficult.
18. He broke .... his holiday.
19. She loves to look .... to those days when they first met.
20. Don't look .... that cupboard. There's a secret in it.
21. He always looks .... his younger brother.
22. The ice was too thin so he broke ....
23. Leave it .... your dad. He can do it faster.
24. Can you help me look .... my ring?
25. Did he give you .... your money yesterday? – No, he didn't. – Never give .... hope!
26. I can't come to your party. I must look .... my little brother.
27. The champion knocked .... the boxer.
28. On Monday I must clean .... the stable.
29. He can't give .... drinking.
30. The truth came ....
31. We are looking .... the holidays.
32. Sit down, Mum! Leave the washing-up .... me!
33. Look .... ! The train is coming!
34. He left her .... the lurch with two little children.
35. Our car broke .... on Friday.

CONDITION: WHAT WOULD YOU DO IF ...?

Study the following sentence pattern (Studiere folgendes Satzmuster):

would + infinitive ⇨ **if + past tense**

Examples: What **would** you **do if** Jack **invited** you for dinner?
If Jack **invited** me for dinner, I **would be** very happy.
What **would** Laura **do** if Nick **brought** her flowers?
If Nick **brought** her flowers, she **would give** him a kiss.

> Merke: Wenn **If** am **B**eginn des Satzes steht, **B**eistrich setzen.

Fill in the missing forms of the verbs:

1. What would Sally do if you .... (help) her?
2. If mum saw the mess, she .... (be) very angry.
3. I .... (cry) if a spider sat on my hair.
4. What .... (he / do) if he won the big prize?
5. If Ben asked me to go out with him, I .... (be) happy.
6. What would you do if you .... (see) the man again?
7. What .... (Laura / do) if you told her the truth?
8. What would you cook if Bill .... (come)?
9. If I had more money, I .... (buy) a new car.
10. What .... (you / do) if Tom wrote to you?
11. If mum had more time, she .... (do) silk painting.
12. What would Sam do if he .... (lose) his key?
13. If John drank too much, he .... (be) sick.
14. What would father do if he .... (miss) the train?
15. If you found a bag full of gold, what .... (you / do)?
16. If he helped me, I .... (be) very happy.
17. What .... (you / do) if you met the girl of your dreams?
18. If Sarah called me, I .... (be) very happy.
19. If you .... (watch) the horror film, you would be very frightened.
20. How would you help him if you .... (can)?
21. What .... (you / answer) if he asked you?
22. If you .... (forget) your homework, what would your teacher say?
23. If we .... (be) late, what would your parents say to you?
24. What would you do if you .... (see) Bill with Lucy?

HOW TO LINK SENTENCES – CONJUNCTIONS

after	nach
although	obwohl
and	und
because	weil
before	bevor
both ... and	sowohl ... als auch
but	aber
either ... or	entweder ... oder
even though	obwohl
however	jedoch
if	wenn, falls
in order to	um zu
neither ... nor	weder ... noch
nevertheless	trotzdem, dennoch
not only ... but as well/but also	nicht nur ..., sondern auch
or	oder
since	da ja
so, therefore	deshalb
so that	sodass
that	welcher, -e, -es (für Dinge, Tiere, Personen)
that's why	deshalb
though	obwohl
to	um zu
when	als
whereas	wohingegen
which	welcher, -e, -es (für Dinge, Tiere)
while	während
who	welcher, -e, -es (für Personen)

Examples:

1. I don't like tennis. I'm not very good at it.
   I don't like tennis **because** I'm not very good at it.
2. Mary is angry. She can't find her lipstick.
   Mary is angry **because** she can't find her lipstick.

3. I tried to skate. I fell down very often.
   I tried to skate, **but** I fell down very often.
4. We stayed at home. It was too cold.
   We stayed at home **because** it was too cold.
5. We visited Mr Smith. He has two horses.
   We visited Mr Smith, **who** has two horses.
6. Jerry is wearing a hat. It is far too big for him.
   Jerry is wearing a hat **that / which** is far too big for him.
7. I have got an exam. I'm very nervous.
   Before an exam I'm very nervous.
   If I have got an exam, I'm very nervous.
8. You cross the road. You must look carefully.
   Before you cross the road, you must look carefully.
9. It is very late. I'm very tired. I'm going to bed now.
   It is very late **and** I'm very tired, **so** I'm going to bed now.
   As it is very late **and** I'm very tired, I'm going to bed now.
   Since it is very late **and** I'm very tired, I'm going to bed now.
10. It is raining. I'm going out.
    It is raining, **but** I'm going out.
    Although it is raining, I'm going out.
    Even though it is raining, I'm going out.
    Though it is raining, I'm going out.
    It is raining; **nevertheless** I'm going out.
11. It is snowing heavily. I'm staying at home.
    It is snowing heavily, **so** I'm staying at home.
    It is snowing heavily, **that's why** I'm staying at home.
    As / Since it is snowing heavily, I'm staying at home.
    I'm staying at home **because** it is snowing heavily.
12. Peter's girlfriend is nice and pretty. She is very helpful.
    Peter's girlfriend is **not only** nice and pretty **but also** very helpful.
    Peter's girlfriend is **not only** nice and pretty **but** very helpful **as well**.
13. Bob doesn't like hamburgers. He ate one.
    Bob doesn't like hamburgers; **nevertheless** he ate one.
    Even though Bob doesn't like hamburgers, he ate one.
14. The weather was unpleasant. It was very cold.
    The weather was **both** unpleasant **and** very cold.
    The weather was **not only** unpleasant **but** very cold **as well**.
    The weather was **not only** unpleasant **but also** very cold.
15. Tommy was late for dinner. Sue was late for dinner.
    Both Tommy **and** Sue were late for dinner.
    Achtung! Das Verb steht in der Mehrzahl!

16. Mary didn't go to the party. Rick didn't go to the party.
    Neither Mary **nor** Rick went to the party.
    Achtung! Das Verb wird nicht mehr verneint! Neither ... nor ist bereits die Verneinung!
17. Cindy doesn't like spinach. Nelly doesn't like spinach.
    Neither Cindy **nor** Nelly likes spinach.
    Achtung! Das Verb steht in der Einzahl!
18. I am hungry. I didn't eat much in the morning.
    I am hungry **because** I didn't eat much in the morning.
    Since / As I didn't eat much in the morning, I am hungry.
19. The children were late. Their father was angry.
    The children were late, **that's why** their father was angry.
    As the children were late, their father was angry.
    Their father was angry **because** the children were late.
20. Would you like to go to McDonald's? Would you like to go to the Happy Chinese?
    Would you like to go to McDonald's **or** to the Happy Chinese?
21. We can go to a fast food restaurant. We can go to a pizzeria.
    We can go **either** to a fast food restaurant **or** to a pizzeria.
22. I was up in my room. Pit called me.
    I was up in my room **when** Pit called me.
23. Mother is knitting. The baby is sleeping.
    While mother is knitting the baby is sleeping.
24. The Ford was expensive. The Opel was more expensive.
    The Ford was expensive, **but** the Opel was more expensive.
    The Ford was expensive; the Opel, **however**, was more expensive.
25. Our new house is very big. It is comfortable.
    Our new house is **not only** very big, **but** (it is) comfortable **as well**.
    Our new house is **not only** very big, **but** (it is) **also** comfortable.
26. Linda is small. Her brother is tall.
    Linda is small, **but** her brother is tall.
    Linda is small **whereas** her brother is tall.
27. Olivia studies hard. She wants to get a good mark.
    Olivia studies hard **in order to** get a good mark.
    Olivia studies hard **because** she wants to get a good mark.
28. Bill ran very fast. He was able to reach the underground.
    Bill ran very fast **so that** he was able to reach the underground.
29. Jimmy had a long night. He was tired.
    After the long night, Jimmy was tired.
30. It is very hot. We jump into the swimming pool.
    It is very hot, **that's why** we jump into the swimming pool.

CONJUNCTIONS

Link the following sentences (Sometimes there are several possibilities):

1. I am waiting for the doctor. I am reading a book.
2. I bought a bottle of sparkling wine. I didn't drink it.
3. Did Milly go out last night? Did she stay at home?
4. Should we walk? Should we call a taxi?
5. I must shut the window. It is too windy.
6. It was cold. We didn't go swimming.
7. Think carefully. Answer the question.
8. You don't run. You won't catch the bus.
9. What's the name of the river? It flows through Linz.
10. Yesterday I saw a woman on TV. She could speak seven languages.
11. Linda is wearing a shirt. It is far too long for her.
12. Mrs Miller came in. She was pale in the face.
13. Liz wants to have new jeans. She wants to have a new pullover.
14. Tom doesn't like popcorn. Nick doesn't like popcorn.
15. You can have a sandwich. You can have toast.
16. Tony wanted to carry his bike. He was too weak.
17. Stella was tired. She went to bed.
18. My summer coat was expensive. My winter coat was even more expensive.
19. The exam was not easy. Bob was able to pass it.
20. Eve studied a lot. She wanted to get a good report.
21. Pamela is short and slim. Her brother is tall and fat.
22. Nora can't go to Pit's party. Lynn can't go to his party.
23. I can't buy a new car. I haven't got any money.
24. It was rainy and stormy. They went for a walk.
25. I feel tired. I didn't sleep much last night.
26. Roger left home at five. He wanted to catch the six o'clock train.
27. We can go to the Greek restaurant. We can got to the Italian restaurant.
28. Her new friend is very charming. He is nice and polite.
29. I wanted to bake a cake. There wasn't any flour left.
30. We can buy a book for her. We can buy flowers.
31. She was very nasty to him. He loves her.
32. Study harder. You won't pass the exam.
33. This is the black dog. It bit Sandra yesterday.
34. She doesn't eat much. She wants to slim.
35. She has got a headache. She is going to bed.
36. She is very nice. Everybody likes her.

37. I had a very big meal. I was tired.
38. I helped him so much. He was very unfriendly to me.
39. We can spend our holidays in Greece. We can spend them in Turkey.
40. You may go out now. Don't be late for dinner.
41. I don't like pork. I don't like beef.
42. You jump into the pond. You must see if it's deep enough.
43. Sue studies hard. She wants to pass her driving licence.
44. It is too late. We can't visit him.
45. I bought a new dress. It's too tight.
46. She is a very good mother. She is a very good cook.
47. Will you come at eight? Will you come at nine?
48. She has got nice flowers in her garden. She looks after them every day.
49. Mother is preparing dinner. The children are doing their homework.
50. It was very late. He called her.
51. This is Mr Funny. He has got a pink car.
52. Milly likes spinach. Bob doesn't like it.
53. He is very poor. He is happy.
54. Jim is angry. He can't find his purse.
55. Sally wanted to be alone. She went up a mountain.
56. I had no dinner. I woke up and was hungry.
57. Tom had a long ride. He was tired.
58. She is very nice to him. He loves her.
59. I don't want a new dress. I don't want a new hat.
60. He hurried. He wanted to meet her at the airport.
61. His girlfriend left him. He is so sad.
62. Eve is very nice and charming. Her sister is arrogant and unfriendly.
63. We didn't see the accident. Our neighbours didn't see it.
64. She got a nice birthday present. She is so happy.
65. Nick is older than his brother. He stays up late.
66. Peter has to study for his exam. He must stay at home.
67. I don't like Charlie. He isn't very nice.
68. We can invite her for dinner. We can invite her for lunch.
69. You can have a lemonade. You can have a Coke.
70. The exam was very difficult. Lisa failed.
71. Go to bed. Brush your teeth.
72. He broke the window. His mother wasn't angry with him.
73. This is Mrs Chatterbox. She knows everything about everybody.
74. Don't tell her anything. She can't keep a secret.
75. I have got an exam. I can't eat anything.
76. This is the new bag. I bought it yesterday.
77. You don't make many mistakes. You are happy.

PRESENT PERFECT TENSE SIMPLE

We use the **present perfect tense** to express **a connection between past and present** (um eine Verbindung zwischen Vergangenheit und Gegenwart auszudrücken).
The action **started in the past and reaches up to the present** or its **effects, its results** reach up to the present. (Die Handlung begann in der Vergangenheit und dauert bis in die Gegenwart oder ihre Auswirkungen, Resultate dauern in der Gegenwart noch an.)

1. Formation: **have / has + past partciple** (3. Zeitwortform)

2. Signal words:

today	
this week, month, year	
so far	*bisher, bis jetzt*
up to now	*bisher, bis jetzt*
just	*gerade*
ever, never	*jemals, niemals*
yet	*noch, schon* (Fragesätze)
not yet	*noch nicht*
recently	*vor Kurzem, neulich*
lately	*in letzter Zeit*
already	*schon* (Aussagesätze)
often	
always	
for	*seit, lang* **(Zeitstrecke)**
since	*seit* **(Zeitpunkt)**

FOR (Zeitstrecke): **for** a second, **for** a minute, **for** an hour, **for** a day, **for** a week, **for** a month, **for** a year, **for** a decade *(ein Jahrzehnt lang)*, **for** a century *(ein Jahrhundert lang)*, **for** ages *(eine Ewigkeit lang)*, **for** a long time ...

SINCE (Zeitpunkt): **since** three o'clock, **since** Monday, **since** last weekend, **since** May, **since** last year, **since** summer 2017, **since** Christmas, **since** Easter, **since** 2018, **since** my youth, **since** breakfast, **since** lunch, **since** dinner, **since** the beginning, **since** my last birthday, **since** when ...

Examples:

Have you *ever* **been** to Paris?
Bist du jemals in Paris gewesen?

He **has eaten** six sandwiches. ***Now he feels sick***. (Resultat)
Er hat sechs Sandwiches gegessen. Nun ist ihm schlecht.

(For) how long **have** you **known** him?
Wie lange *kennst du ihn schon*?
Achtung! Manche deutschen *schon-Sätze* stehen in der Gegenwart!

He **has** *just* **come** back.
Er ist soeben / gerade zurückgekommen.

She **has been** here *since* 2 o'clock.
Sie *ist schon* seit zwei Uhr hier.

She **has lived** in Vienna *for* a year. She likes it there.
Sie *lebt schon* seit einem Jahr in Wien. Es gefällt ihr dort.

She **has** *never* **seen** such a nice picture.
Sie hat noch nie so ein schönes Bild gesehen.

I**'ve been** in Austria *since* my youth.
Ich *bin schon* seit meiner Jugend in Österreich.

She **has been** there *since* she was a baby.
Sie *ist schon* dort seit sie ein Baby war.

I **have** *already* **done** my homework. (kein Fragesatz, sondern Aussagesatz mit *already*)
Ich habe meine Hausübung schon / bereits gemacht.

Have you **done** your homework *yet*? (Fragesatz mit *yet*)
Hast du deine Hausübung schon gemacht?

No, I **haven't done** it *yet*. (verneinter Satz mit *yet*)
Nein, ich habe sie noch nicht gemacht.

PAST PARTICIPLE

be	was	**been**
become	became	**become**
begin	began	**begun**
bite	bit	**bitten**
blow	blew	**blown**
break	broke	**broken**
bring	brought	**brought**
build	built	**built**
buy	bought	**bought**
can	could	**have / has been able to**
catch	caught	**caught**
choose	chose	**chosen**
come	came	**come**
cost	cost	**cost**
cut	cut	**cut**
dig	dug	**dug**
do	did	**done**
draw	drew	**drawn**
drink	drank	**drunk**
drive	drove	**driven**
eat	ate	**eaten**
fall	fell	**fallen**
feed	fed	**fed**
feel	felt	**felt**
fight	fought	**fought**
find	found	**found**
flee	fled	**fled**
fly	flew	**flown**
forget	forgot	**forgotten**
freeze	froze	**frozen**
get	got	**got**
give	gave	**given**
go	went	**gone**
grow	grew	**grown**
hang	hung	**hung**
have	had	**had**
hear	heard	**heard**
hide	hid	**hid(den)**
hit	hit	**hit**
hold	held	**held**
hurt	hurt	**hurt**
keep	kept	**kept**
know	knew	**known**
lay	laid	**laid**

leave	left	**left**
let	let	**let**
lie	lay	**lain**
lose	lost	**lost**
make	made	**made**
meet	met	**met**
must	had to	**have / has had to**
pay	paid	**paid**
put	put	**put**
read	read	**read**
ring	rang	**rung**
run	ran	**run**
say	said	**said**
see	saw	**seen**
sell	sold	**sold**
send	sent	**sent**
set	set	**set**
shake	shook	**shaken**
shine	shone	**shone**
shoot	shot	**shot**
show	showed	**shown / showed**
shut	shut	**shut**
sing	sang	**sung**
sink	sank	**sunk**
sleep	slept	**slept**
speak	spoke	**spoken**
spend	spent	**spent**
spill	spilt	**spilt**
spring	sprang	**sprung**
stand	stood	**stood**
steal	stole	**stolen**
stink	stank	**stunk**
strike	struck	**struck**
sweep	swept	**swept**
swim	swam	**swum**
take	took	**taken**
teach	taught	**taught**
tear [teə(r)]	tore	**torn**
tell	told	**told**
think	thought	**thought**
throw	threw	**thrown**
wake	woke	**woken**
wear	wore	**worn**
weep	wept	**wept**
win	won	**won**
write	wrote	**written**

FOR   SINCE

1. Clare has worked here in this office .... 2016.
2. She has worked here .... many years.
3. I've not been in Greece .... 15 years.
4. She's lived in Linz .... her youth.
5. It has rained .... three weeks. I'm happy that it has stopped now.
6. It hasn't snowed .... Christmas.
7. I haven't spoken French .... my last holidays.
8. .... how long have you known Mary?
9. We have been in Dublin .... last Friday.
10. He has studied .... three hours. Now he is tired.
11. We haven't met .... eight years.
12. We have had this car .... 2017.
13. I have not eaten chocolates .... two weeks. I'm on a diet.
14. Mary has been ill .... Friday, that is .... eight days.
15. Hi, Larry! I haven't seen you .... a month!
16. I haven't seen him .... Easter.
17. We have been here .... two hours.
18. She has lived in Vienna .... January.
19. She hasn't spoken to me .... more than two months.
20. Pit hasn't eaten any meat .... ages.
21. Sally has not written to me .... many weeks.
22. They haven't sent their daughter any money .... last year.
23. It hasn't rained .... more than a month.
24. I've written three letters .... breakfast.
25. He has not found his key .... this morning.
26. They haven't spoken to each other .... their quarrel.
27. .... when have you been married?
28. My friend has been ill .... a long time.
29. He hasn't done any work .... a month.
30. Bill hasn't visited his uncle .... two years.
31. She hasn't bought any new clothes .... the beginning of the year.
32. You haven't read a book .... more than four weeks.
33. Ken hasn't washed his face .... lunchtime.
34. He has not had a holiday .... 2015!
35. .... how long has she lived there?
36. He hasn't waited .... a long time.
37. He hasn't written to me .... January.
38. She has been in Salzburg .... her youth.

PRESENT PERFECT OR PAST TENSE

1. Granny .... (go) to see the doctor last week.
2. Mr Ronaldo .... (drive) to Rome five times this year.
3. .... (you / meet) Cousin Ann this year?
4. Mother .... (study) French when she was at school.
5. They .... (live) in Salzburg for ten years.
6. Uncle Ben .... (be) in New York last winter.
7. They .... (live) in Oxford from 2015 to 2017.
8. A new pupil .... (be) in our class since Easter.
9. I .... (see) Tom and Jerry a few minutes ago.
10. My girlfriend .... (work) in Paris last year.
11. I .... (never see) a real monster.
12. I can't find my keys. .... (you / see) them?
13. Perhaps I .... (leave) them in the car last night.
14. The baby .... (cry) four times today.
15. .... (you / meet / him) yet?
16. Peter .... (must) go to the dentist's the week before last.
17. I .... (go) to the cinema twice this month.
18. .... (you / see) Mr Hall today?
19. Yesterday I .... (must) wait for the next bus for a long time because I .... (miss) one.
20. She .... (finish) her homework half an hour ago.
21. I .... (read) this book some years ago.
22. The bus .... (not yet / arrive).
23. Sally .... (just / switch on) the radio.
24. Charlie .... (give up) smoking last year.
25. Some years ago Basil .... (have) a car accident.
26. Last week Frank .... (be) at our house, but I .... (not see) him since then.
27. .... (you / be) to the doctor's yet?
28. When we .... (go) shopping to town we .... (meet) Sandy and Liz in front of a shop.
29. I .... (buy) this dress last winter.
30. We .... (not visit) Peter since Easter.
31. They .... (not be) to the funfair for years.
32. When .... (you / write) this letter? – I .... (write) it last week.
33. She .... (meet) him in town some days ago.

34. Are you hungry? – No, thanks, I .... (just / have) a sandwich.
35. Rick .... (not drink) any alcohol for more than three years.
36. .... (you / read) the latest Tom Turbo yet? – No, I .... (not read) it yet but Sue .... (read) it last week. She .... (like) it very much.
37. .... (you / ever / be) to India?
38. We .... (not play) "Uno" for three weeks.
39. He .... (spend) his holidays in Greece last summer.
40. How long .... (you / have) your Ford? – I .... (buy) it last spring so I .... (have) it for half a year.
41. They .... (just / bring) the new piano.
42. Since when .... (he / be) here? – He .... (come) yesterday.
43. Many Americans .... (never / be) to Austria.
44. .... (you / sleep) well last night?
45. I .... (not see) the new science fiction film yet.
46. Susan is ill. How long .... (she / be) ill? – For two weeks.
47. Last year she .... (be) ill for two months.
48. What time .... (you / have) breakfast this morning? At eight.
49. I .... (not have) anything to eat since eight.
50. .... (you / ever / be) to Denmark? – Yes, I .... (be) there in the summer of 2017.
51. I .... (lose) my keys. – .... (you / see) them?
52. Where .... (you / spend) your holidays in 2016?
53. Grandpa .... (go) to see the dentist yesterday. He .... (have) a toothache since last week.
54. .... (you / read) this book? – Yes, I .... (read) it during the holidays.
55. How long ago .... (you / arrive) here?
56. I .... (not play) the violin since last winter.
57. Our family .... (finish) breakfast ten minutes ago.
58. .... (you / see) the moon last night?
59. Tina .... (wash) her hair. It is wet now.
60. Sandy .... (post) the letter yesterday.
61. Sue .... (not see) the latest film with Tom Hanks yet.
62. Mother .... (already / try on) her new dress.

63. The pupil .... (work) in the library since 8 o'clock.
64. He .... (be) there from eight to ten.
65. Yesterday we .... (listen) to his interesting tales.
66. .... (you / meet) Tom lately? – No, we .... (not meet) since April.
67. We .... (work) much this week.
68. We .... (work) much two weeks ago.
69. We .... (have) a lot of snow last winter.
70. Charles .... (go) to London in 2017.
71. Bobby .... (not be) to Italy since last holidays.
72. They .... (not arrive) yet.
73. Why .... (you / not answer) the phone? I .... (call) you at eight.
74. The Wagners .... (not have) a holiday for two years.
75. When .... (you / wake up)?
76. The children .... (play) in the playground for two hours. They are quite dirty now.
77. You look funny! – I .... (just / wake) up!
78. Mum .... (sweep) the floor two hours ago! Look what you .... (do)! It is dirty again!
79. Grandma .... (be) here for one day. She is going to stay for two weeks.
80. He .... (hurt) her last year. Since then she .... (hate) him.
81. Where is Jim? – He .... (go) on a holiday. – Oh, that's why he isn't here.
82. It .... (rain). Look, the streets are wet.
83. Liz .... (never be) to France.
84. Phil .... (go) there when he was fourteen.
85. I'm sorry, I .... (never learn) to play the piano, but my brother .... (learn) it when he was six.
86. She .... (already / bake) the cake for his birthday.
87. What .... (happen)? You're bleeding!
88. .... (you / drink) your tea yet? – No, it .... (be) too hot.
89. .... (the baker / bring) the bread yet? – No, I'm afraid he .... (not have).
90. Sue .... (return) the books two days ago.
91. They .... (move) to Vienna last year.
92. Harry .... (take) ten driving lessons two weeks ago.
93. .... (your parents / be) to Greece last year? – No, they .... (not be) there.

94. .... (you / see) him lately? — No, we .... (not meet) since his birthday.
95. I .... (not be) to Jesolo since I .... (be) four years old.
96. Frank .... (not be) to the cinema for three months.
97. Mother .... (go) shopping three days ago.
98. .... (she / borrow) some money from you last week? — Yes, but she .... (not yet / return) it to me.
99. They .... (not have) a meeting since they .... (leave) university in 2010.
100. How long .... (they / live) in this nice flat? — For five years. They .... (buy) it when Simon .... (be) a baby.
101. .... (you / ever / see) the sea? — Yes, three times. I first .... (go) there when I .... (be) a little boy.
102. .... (you / have) time to talk to her since you .... (arrive) yesterday? — No, I .... (not yet / talk) to anybody since I .... (come) to her house.
103. .... (it / rain) during your stay in Cornwall? — No, it .... (be) bright and warm. — When .... (you / come) back? — Yesterday.
104. They .... (be) afraid of ghosts since they .... (be) at the old castle.
105. For how long .... (you / have) this brilliant idea? — Since yesterday.
106. Oh, no! Look what you .... (do)! You .... (spill) your hot chocolate all over your new T-shirt!
107. She .... (forget) to water the flowers last week.
108. I'm awfully tired because I .... (work) a lot for my English test.
109. I .... (understand) all the rules since she .... (explain) them to us.
110. Do you understand the present perfect tense? — Oh yes, everything .... (be) clear to me from the beginning.
111. I .... (not have) any difficulties at all ever since we .... (talk) about present perfect last week.
112. Sally .... (not finish) her homework yet.
113. Sue .... (do) it half an hour ago.
114. When .... (he / come) ? — He .... (arrive) at six.

115. Up to now he .... (never see) a yellow elephant.
116. .... (you / drink) too much last night?
117. Mr Miller .... (just / leave) his office.
118. Our neighbour's cat .... (be) run over by a car yesterday.
119. .... (you / wear) your hair long when you .... (be) at school, Dad? – No, I .... (wear) it short.
120. He .... (break) his leg in June.
   He .... (not can) go out since then.
121. Our train .... (not yet / arrive).
122. I .... (not see) her for more than two years.
123. My parents .... (just / arrive) from New York.
124. Where .... (you / meet) her for the first time?
125. Alice .... (start) in the office in 2015. Up to now she .... (be) happy there.
126. .... (you / ever / eat) beans on toast? –
   Yes, I .... (eat) them in England last year.
127. Last week they .... (buy) a new car.
128. Ten years ago she .... (leave) school and .... (start) to work.
129. Martin .... (never see) a UFO.
130. She only .... (see) a football match twice before.
131. .... (they / ever / give) you any money? –
   Yes, they .... (give) me some last week.
132. I .... (not watch) TV at all this week.
133. Last week I .... (see) some interesting programmes.
134. .... (you / be) busy at work this month? –
   No, but I .... (be) very busy last month.
135. Hi, Daisy! .... (you / have) a nice day today? –
   No, not really. Yesterday I .... (feel) better and .... (have) more energy than today.
136. Since when .... (Sarah / be) here with you? –
   She .... (arrive) on Friday, so she .... (be) here for six days.
137. He .... (not smoke) for a long time. He is very proud of it.
138. Michael .... (wash) his hands. They are clean now.
139. Mum .... (be) at the hairdresser's from eight to ten on Tuesday.

POSSESSIVE PRONOUNS

Die Possessivpronomen mine, yours, his, hers, its, ours, theirs
werden ohne **Hauptwort** verwendet.
(Der, die, das mein(ig)e/n; der, die, das dein(ig)e/n; sein(ig)e/n; ihr(ig)e/n;
unsr(ig)e/n; eur(ig)e/n)

I	my	*mine*	It looks like my book. Yes, it is **mine**.
you	your	*yours*	This is your pen. It is **yours**.
he	his	*his*	Is this his hat? — Yes it's **his**.
she	her	*hers*	It's her cat. It's **hers**.
it	its	*its*	This is the dog's bone. It's **its**.
we	our	*ours*	These are our trainers. They are **ours**.
you	your	*yours*	Don't eat my sandwich! Eat **yours**!
they	their	*theirs*	Are these their shoes? — Yes, they are **theirs**.

Anmerkung: Bei Haustieren kennt man meistens das Geschlecht des Tieres.
Daher ist auch **his / hers** möglich.

Keep in mind:

He is a friend *of* mine.	*Er ist ein Freund von mir.*
Is this a friend *of* yours?	*Ist das ein Freund von dir?*
They are friends *of* ours.	*Sie sind Freunde von uns.*

1. This is Frank's problem. It is ....
2. Is that their house? — No, ... is at the end of the street.
3. You give us your address and we will give you ....
4. Don't drink this bowl of milk. It's the cat's. It's ....
5. You can have my pencil. Take ....
6. Is this his new camera? — Yes it's ....
7. My coat is old. Her coat is new. .... is old, ... is new.
8. Our party was great. .... was great.
9. It can't be my book. .... is green.
10. It must be his umbrella. .... has got stars.
11. I'm sure this is your key. This is ....
12. I've got my purse in my pocket. Look, ... is in my pocket.
13. Our car is dark green. .... is dark green.
14. They spent their holidays in Greece with some friends ....

PAST TENSE PROGRESSIVE

Formation: was / were + ing-form

It is used:

1)	Für *lang andauernde* Handlungen in der past tense:

The children **were fighting** over a toy car.
He **was waiting for** the train.
The baby **was crying** all afternoon.

2)	Wenn zwei vergangene Handlungen *gleichzeitig* verlaufen:

Father **was reading** the news *while* mother **was writing** a letter.
Simon **was doing** his homework *while* Susan **was playing**.
Mother **was baking** a cake and Pam **was watching** her.

3)	Eine *lange Handlung* wird von einer *kurzen* (meist plötzlich) *unterbrochen*: Die *längere* Handlung steht in der *progressive form*, die *kürzere* in der *simple form*.

They **were eating** *when suddenly* the bell **rang**.
When he **was running** across the street he **fell** down.
He **was sleeping** *when suddenly* mother **entered** the room.

4)	Eine Handlung verlief zu einem *bestimmten* vergangenen *Zeitpunkt*, oder *innerhalb einer genau begrenzten Zeitspanne*:

What **were** you **doing** *yesterday at three o'clock*? –
Yesterday at three? I **was reading**.
On Friday between four and five I **was having** tea with my parents.
Yesterday I **was sleeping** *from three to four* in the afternoon.

PAST PROGRESSIVE OR SIMPLE PAST

1. Sally .... (not be) at home yesterday afternoon. She .... (play) tennis with Norman.
2. She .... (not watch) TV yesterday evening, she .... (read) in bed.
3. What .... (you / do) at 12 o'clock yesterday? – I .... (have) lunch with my family.
4. What .... (he / say) to you? – I don't know. I .... (not listen).
5. It .... (rain) heavily, so we .... (not go) to Uncle Sam yesterday afternoon.
6. In 2017 my girlfriend .... (work) in France.
7. When I .... (wake up) yesterday, the sun .... (shine) brightly.
8. Father .... (still work) at 11:30 last night.
9. They .... (have) dinner while the baby .... (be) asleep.
10. What .... (you / do) at three o'clock yesterday? – I .... (have) tea with my husband.
11. Ann .... (be) at home last night. She .... (watch) her favourite film.
12. Carol .... (watch) her little sister play when the telephone .... (ring).
13. Charles .... (drive) back home from work at 6 p.m. yesterday evening.
14. Nora .... (be) at the station at four yesterday. She .... (wait) for the train to Linz.
15. The Bancrofts .... (take) their dog for a walk in the park at three o'clock yesterday.
16. At nine in the morning Sheila .... (wash) her car.
17. From one to two she .... (have) a bath in the swimming pool.
18. I .... (not / can) hear the telephone, the baby .... (cry).
19. What .... (Tom / do) when you .... (meet) him? – He .... (shop).
20. What .... (Tina / wear) to school yesterday?
21. .... (it / rain) when you .... (take) dad to the airport?

22. Father .... (read) his newspaper while mother .... (knit).
23. What .... (he / do) when the light .... (go) out in the house? — He .... (try) to change a bulb.
24. When I .... (see) Mrs Moon she .... (carry) two heavy boxes.
25. When I .... (see) the thief yesterday he .... (wear) a blue coat and .... (carry) two bags.
26. While he .... (be) on his way to town he .... (smoke) a pipe.
27. What .... (John / do) when the telephone .... (ring)? — He .... (hang up) a picture.
28. .... (you / watch) a horror film on TV when I .... (call) you yesterday evening? — No, little Sue .... (cry).
29. Yesterday I .... (start) work at 7 and .... (stop) at six.
30. When we .... (go) for a walk, it .... (snow) heavily yesterday afternoon.
31. I .... (see) Mrs Brown and Mrs Miller. They .... (wait) at the bus stop.
32. She .... (fall) asleep while she .... (read) a boring book.
33. Jack .... (count) his badges when his friend .... (come) round.
34. Mr Sparkling .... (walk) down the street, when he .... (meet) his old friend Bill.
35. They .... (sit) on the veranda, when it .... (start) to rain.
36. They .... (have) a party when the fire .... (break) out in the kitchen.
37. When Sharon .... (hang up) the new curtains in the living room she .... (fall) off the ladder.
38. Pam .... (break) her toes when she .... (slip) on a banana peel.
39. Frank .... (not be) hungry, so he .... (leave) without breakfast.

40. Stella .... (not be) at home when I .... (go) to see her.
41. Yesterday I .... (get up) early. I .... (brush) my teeth, ... (comb) my hair and then I .... (have) a rich breakfast.
42. The postman .... (bring) a telegram while we .... (have) lunch.
43. We .... (meet) Julian at the party. He .... (wear) a dark suit.
44. I .... (read) the newspaper while I .... (wait) for the doctor.
45. She .... (fall out) of her bed while she .... (have) a nightmare.
46. Sally .... (have) a chat with Sue while her father .... (watch) TV.
47. Somebody .... (steal) Linda's bike yesterday. .... (you / see) anything?
48. The boys .... (break) Mrs Smith's window when they .... (play) basketball.
49. Oliver .... (wait) for his father when he .... (return) from work.
50. The boy .... (fall) down when he .... (run) after the cat.
51. I .... (get up) at seven. The weather .... (be) so fine that I .... (take) a walk in the fresh air.
52. Frank Simons .... (not drive) too fast when suddenly the accident .... (happen) an hour ago.
53. Pamela .... (not go) to work yesterday. She .... (be) ill. She .... (have) a cold.
54. What .... (you / do) at nine on Saturday evening?
55. Poor Jimmy .... (lose) his bus ticket when he .... (run) after the bus.
56. While Susan .... (do) her homework little Tommy .... (try) to disturb her.
57. .... (she / wear) her new dress when you .... (see) her at the concert yesterday?
58. When he .... (go) into the kitchen he .... (see) that his mother .... (bake) a cake.
59. When Rose .... (open) the door the neighbour .... (wait) with flowers in his hands.
60. While the students .... (walk) home from the party they .... (sing) loudly and happily.

61. I have no idea what they .... (talk) about yesterday. I .... (not hear) anything.
62. She .... (look) at her daughter who .... (play) with her doll.
63. When he .... (see) the pretty girl he .... (smile) at her in a friendly way.
64. The little boy .... (listen) to granny's story when he suddenly .... (begin) to weep.
65. They .... (sit) in the living room when they, all of a sudden, ... (hear) the noise.
66. We .... (travel) through France when we .... (meet) the Smiths.
67. He .... (ride) his bike across the field when it suddenly .... (get) a flat tyre.
68. Father .... (wash) the dishes while mother .... (feed) little Alan.
69. She .... (wash) her hair when her friends .... (come) to see her.
70. They .... (look out) of the window because it .... (snow) heavily.
71. We .... (have) tea at four when the postman .... (bring) a letter.
72. Tim .... (hide) behind the door of the living room to hear what his parents .... (talk) about.
73. The children .... (not hear) the telephone because they .... (play) in the garden.
74. What .... (he / do) at this time yesterday? – He .... (cut) the grass.
75. Yesterday afternoon they .... (sit) in the garden when the storm .... (break).
76. He .... (have) a bath when the bell .... (ring).
77. I .... (phone) you four times between two and three yesterday. Where .... (you / be)? – I .... (shop).
78. Last Saturday Tracy .... (sunbathe) the whole afternoon.
79. Yesterday afternoon I .... (pick) the children up from school. Then I .... (drive) to granny's place and .... (bring) her some medicine.
80. They .... (talk) to their neighbours in the garden when the thunderstorm .... (break).

81. Last Wednesday we .... (play) football from seven to eight.
82. Last Friday morning I .... (read) a book when Sheila suddenly .... (knock) at the door.
83. Last weekend we .... (walk) in the mountains when Sue .... (fall) over a stone and .... (hurt) her leg.
84. You .... (wear) a new hat when I .... (meet) you in town yesterday.
85. When Peter .... (swim) in the lake he suddenly .... (hear) a scream. It .... (be) Bill, who .... (watch) something green in the lake and .... (think) it .... (be) a crocodile.
86. When I .... (meet) Phil last week, he .... (ride) his new mountain bike.
87. We .... (talk) about the wonderful summer evening, when suddenly there .... (be) a thunderstorm.
88. While we .... (watch) a video, Sam .... (listen) to his favourite pop group.
89. While Mr Grant .... (pay) a visit to his mother, somebody .... (break) into his house and .... (steal) a painting.
90. While the children .... (build) castles in the sand, father .... (surf).
91. While they .... (have) breakfast, Mr Stevens .... (read) the Morning Post.
92. While mum .... (write) a letter to Aunt Maggie, Betty .... (make) a phone call.
93. While Helen .... (tidy up) her room, Betty .... (ring) her up and .... (tell) her about Rick's party.
94. She .... (do) her homework when Pat .... (enter) the room.
95. While dad .... (pack) his suitcase, Ann .... (help) in the kitchen.
96. He .... (stand) under this statue when I .... (take) the photograph.
97. It .... (rain) in the morning when I .... (get) up.
98. They .... (live) in Switzerland when the Second World War .... (break) out.

99. Molly and Jerry .... (sit) in a restaurant when I .... (see) them.
100. He .... (play) his favourite record when I .... (come) to see him.
101. We .... (have) supper when we .... (hear) a terrible noise.
102. The boy .... (do) his homework when his mother .... (ask) him to come.
103. While John .... (repair) the garden bench Mary .... (iron) the tablecloth.
104. I .... (have) a bath when the guests .... (arrive).
105. Many people .... (wait) at the station when the Scorpions .... (arrive).
106. Tom .... (play) the piano, mum .... (work) in the kitchen and dad .... (repair) Eric's bike.
107. We .... (have) tea when the candle .... (set) the tablecloth on fire.
108. Just as Ben .... (leave), the telephone .... (ring). He .... (must) go back into the living room to answer the phone.
109. While dad .... (shave), he .... (cut) himself.
110. Tom .... (bleed) so heavily that mother .... (take) him to the hospital.
111. While Sandy .... (play) the guitar Linda .... (listen) to her.
112. Somebody .... (steal) my bike while I .... (swim) in the lake.
113. He .... (walk) in the park when suddenly the wind .... (blow) his hat off.
114. I .... (have) a computer course from five to six yesterday.
115. What .... (they / do) at 11 yesterday? They .... (play) squash, as far as I know.
116. This time last year we .... (spend) our holidays in Greece.
117. Mother .... (cook) when she .... (burn) her right hand.
118. While Mr Frances .... (water) the flowers in the garden, he .... (hurt) his back.

119. I .... (see) Danny in the park. He .... (sit) in the grass and .... (listen) to his MP3 player.
120. When Phil .... (come) we .... (have) tea.
121. At 9 o'clock mum .... (have) breakfast.
122. Daniel .... (want) to go out when his brother .... (ask) him to stay and help him with the homework.
123. When we .... (walk) home it .... (begin) to rain.
124. We .... (wait) for the taxi when the child suddenly .... (run) across the street without looking.
125. Trish .... (fall) off the ladder when she .... (paint) the walls of her new flat.
126. Last night I .... (read) in bed when suddenly I .... (hear) a scream. I .... (get) out of bed and .... (look) out of the window. A cat .... (cry) in front of my window.
127. I .... (have) a shower when the TV set .... (explode).
128. Mary .... (do) the washing-up when a cup .... (slip) out of her hand and .... (crash) onto the floor.
129. Fred .... (take) a slice of cake while I .... (not look).
130. I .... (see) Pam at Roger's party yesterday. She .... (wear) a long, black and elegant dress.
131. From two to three I .... (must) study, but the neighbour's dog .... (bark) all the time.
132. This time last year I .... (be) in Greece.
133. When Aunt Liz .... (come) we .... (show) her our house.
134. It was boring. They .... (talk) about their holidays all the time.
135. While she .... (have) a chat on the phone, her cake .... (burn) in the oven.
136. In August last year he .... (study) for his driving test.
137. Tom and Sue .... (pick) flowers while mum .... (get) ready for a walk.
138. Rick .... (watch) the clouds pass by when a bird .... (drop) a worm on his head.

LOTS (OF)   A LOT (OF)   MUCH   MANY

Lots (of) = a lot (of) (*viel / viele / vieles*) wird in der <u>modernen Alltagssprache</u> verwendet. Das Verb wird **je nach Grundwort** im *Singular* oder *Plural* eingesetzt.
In **Frage und Verneinung** wird <u>auch</u> **much / many** gebraucht.

1.	Mit Verb im Singular bei *unzählbaren* Ausdrücken:

There *is* **lots of rum** in this cake.
There *is* **lots more** I can tell you.
There *is* **lots of milk** in your coffee.
There *is* **a lot of water** in the bowl.

2.	Mit Verb im Plural bei *zählbaren* Ausdrücken:

There *are* **lots of book<u>s</u>** on the table.
There *are* **a lot of book<u>s</u>** on the shelf.
Lots of apple<u>s</u> *were* on the ground.
There *were* **lots of pear<u>s</u>** in the basket.
A lot of friend<u>s</u> *were* at the party.
Lots of friend<u>s</u> *were* there.
A lot of science fiction book<u>s</u> *are* in his desk.
Lots of science fiction book<u>s</u> *were* very thrilling.

3.	Much / many in *Frage* und *Verneinung*:

I do**n't** eat **much** meat.
Do you drink **much** alcohol?
We have**n't** got **much** time.
I have **never** had **much** money.
Do you get **much** pocket money?
I do**n't** eat **many** sweets.

PRESENT TENSE WITH CERTAIN TIME EXPRESSIONS

Always use PRESENT TENSE with the following time expressions:

as soon as
until / till
after
when　　　　　　　to express **FUTURE** ACTIONS
before
while

(Um **zukünftige** Handlungen auszudrücken, darfst du mit den **obigen Zeitbestimmungen** nur die **present simple tense** verwenden und **nicht** die **Zukunft**!)

Study the following examples:

We'll look for your key *until* we **find** it.
I'll ask him *as soon as* he **comes**.
They will tell her everything *when* they **see** her.
When I**'m** in town I'll meet her.
I'll be sad *when* she **leaves**.
He will help me *while* he **is** here.
I'll give you my address *before* you **go**.
I'll see you later *when* I **have** more time.
We will meet you *when* we **are** back again.
Will you please close the windows *before* you **go** out?
She is going to see after our house *while* we **are** away.
I'll stay here *until* you **come** back.
Would you like something to eat *before* you **leave**?
When I **grow** up, I want to be an astronaut.
When I **come** home this evening, I'm going to have a nice meal.
When I**'m** in Paris, I'm going to visit the Eiffel Tower.
Wait here *until* the rain **is** over.

MODAL VERBS IN PRESENT PERFECT TENSE

CAN I **have been able to** solve the riddle. Look!
She **has been able to** bake her first cake now.

CANNOT Up to now I **have not been able to (haven't been able to / have been unable to)** finish the letter.
She **hasn't been able to** cook lunch.

MAY I **have been allowed to** drink a glass of wine.
He **has been allowed to** watch TV.

MUST NOT We **have not been allowed to** see the film tonight.
He **hasn't been allowed to** go to the cinema for a week.

MUST I **have had to** help mother for two hours now.
She **has had to** wash the dishes until now.

NEEDN'T I **haven't had to** wait for her for a long time.
She **hasn't had to** do her homework now.

1. I .... (must) work a lot this afternoon. Now I'm tired.
2. He .... (can) help her for more than a year now.
3. .... (she / may) use your bike this morning?
4. Up to now I .... (cannot) find the answer to this problem.
5. I .... (needn't) pay the new windows since they built them in last month.
6. She .... (must not) drink coffee since her stomachache.
7. Larry .... (must) stay in bed for two weeks now.
   He .... (must not) get up.
8. We .... (cannot) leave the house for a week now because we all have got the flu.
9. .... (you / can) do this exercise?

MIXED TENSES

1. .... (you / be) to the dentist's yet? —
   Yes, I .... (be) there yesterday afternoon.
2. Sue .... (wear) her new dark blue dress tomorrow evening.
3. She .... (meet) him in the park two weeks ago.
4. I .... (must) wait for Ronald for two hours.
   I .... (be) happy that he .... (be) here now!
5. The Millers .... (buy) a new piano the next days.
6. He .... (be) forty next Monday. —
   We .... (have) a nice party.
7. Look, they .... (bring) the Smiths' new furniture.
8. Don't forget to post the birthday card for Aunt Mary! — But I .... (already post) it, Mum!
9. I .... (cannot) draw a picture since my last holidays.
10. Peter and Tom .... (already do) their homework, so they .... (may) watch TV now.
11. What .... (the boys / do) ? —
    They .... (watch) an interesting film on insects.
12. Oh, no! What a mess! Look what you .... (do)!
    You .... (break) my new mirror! —
    I .... (be) so sorry!
    I .... (buy) a new one tomorrow.
13. Please inform me as soon as Peter .... (call) tomorrow.
    I'm going to wait till he .... (phone).
14. When .... (you / last / see) her? — Let me .... (think). I .... (meet) her at Frank's party.
    That .... (be) last Wednesday.
15. The tunnel .... (be) built a long time ago.
16. Where .... (you / spend) your next holidays?
    In France again? — No, we .... (go) there last year.
    This year we .... (fly) to Greece, because we .... (not be) there for ages!
17. Harry .... (never be) to Rome, but he .... (go) there next summer.
18. Yesterday we .... (visit) the museum.
    It .... (be) very interesting.

19. The test tomorrow .... (not be) difficult for us because we .... (study) a lot.
20. It .... (snow) a lot. Now the streets .... (be) white.
21. Look, it .... (still snow)! We .... (make) a big snow castle!
22. .... (you / often / see) him? — No, we rarely .... (meet). I .... (not see) him for ages.
23. .... (you / often / see) him last year? — No, we rarely .... (meet). He .... (be) so busy.
24. The grass and the trees .... (be) dry. It .... (not rain) for five weeks. I hope it .... (rain) soon.
25. She .... (finish) the exercise sheet. Now she .... (be) happy.
26. She .... (not can) do her homework for more than an hour. She .... (still sit) over it.
27. Peter .... (not may) go to Fred's party tomorrow. He .... (must) look after his little sister.
28. There .... (be) a meeting of the Fishermen's Club on Friday 8 p.m.
29. I think I .... (have) an ice cream soda now.
30. While the dog .... (sleep) a man .... (jump) over the garden fence.
31. Give me the key before you .... (go), please.
32. Fine! It .... (be) sunny and hot the next weekend. We .... (have) a boat ride.
33. What .... (you / knit) now? — A pullover. — This time last year you .... (knit) a jacket for Jim.
34. As soon as he .... (get) the money he .... (buy) a ring for her.
35. I .... (never drink) gin so far. I think I .... (never try) it.
36. Dad .... (not smoke) much last month. He .... (probably give up) smoking.
37. What .... (you / do) during the last hour? — First I .... (call) Dave, then I .... (prepare) dinner, then I .... (take) the dog for a walk.
38. You .... (must) work very much this year. Now you .... (know) lots of new things. I hope you .... (enjoy) your holidays!

WORDS

absence	*Abwesenheit*	cloth	*Stoff*
accident	*Unfall*	come round	*besuchen*
advice	*Rat*	completely	*total, komplett*
airport	*Flugplatz*	composition	*Aufsatz*
alone	*allein*	confess	*zugeben*
anthem (national)	*Landeshymne*	contact	*kontaktieren*
applaud	*applaudieren*	copy	*abschreiben*
arrogant	*arrogant*	country	*Land*
athlete	*Athlet*	crash	*krachen*
attic	*Dachboden*	crash into	*anfahren*
awake	*wach*	date	*Treffen*
balcony	*Balkon*	death	*Tod*
bear	*Bär*	Denmark	*Dänemark*
beef	*Rindfleisch*	diet	*Diät*
behave	*sich benehmen*	dig	*graben*
bench	*Bank*	dirty	*schmutzig*
bet	*wetten*	dislike	*nicht mögen*
boots	*Stiefel*	disturb	*stören*
bowl	*Schale*	do you mind	*hast du was dagegen*
break down	*kaputt werden*		
breathe in	*einatmen*	dress	*sich anziehen; Kleid*
broke	*pleite; brach*	dressed	*gekleidet*
broken	*zerbrochen*	driver	*Lenker*
bulb	*Glühbirne*	driving licence	*Führerschein*
bully	*Tyrann, Rabauke*	driving test	*Fahrprüfung*
burglar	*Einbrecher*	drop	*fallen lassen*
busy	*beschäftigt*	during	*während*
calm down	*sich beruhigen*	earn	*verdienen*
candle	*Kerze*	elbow	*Ellbogen*
care for	*sich kümmern um*	energy	*Energie*
Carinthia	*Kärnten*	enjoy	*gerne tun / haben*
carpet	*Teppich*	enough	*genug*
carry	*tragen*	everything	*alles*
change	*wechseln*	exciting	*aufregend*
charity	*Wohltätigkeits-*	expect	*erwarten*
charming	*charmant*	explode	*explodieren*
chat	*plaudern; Tratsch*	fact	*Tatsache*
cheeky	*frech*	fail	*nicht bestehen*
chemist's	*Apotheke*	fashionably	*modisch*
chess	*Schach*	fear	*(be)fürchten*
Chinese	*chinesisch*	fence	*Zaun*
choose	*auswählen*	fetch	*holen, bringen*
chose	*wählte aus*	fight	*kämpfen, streiten*
closed	*geschlossen*	fight over	*streiten um*

finished	*aus, beendet*	leave	*verlassen*
flee	*fliehen*	left	*übrig; verließ; links*
flow	*fließen*	lend	*borgen*
flu	*Grippe*	let	*lassen*
fly	*fliegen*	library	*Bücherei*
for joy	*vor Freude*	lie	*lügen; Lüge; liegen*
foreign language	*Fremdsprache*	link	*verbinden*
forget	*vergessen*	lion	*Löwe*
freeze	*frieren*	lipstick	*Lippenstift*
friendship	*Freundschaft*	lose	*verlieren*
funfair	*Volksfest*	lost	*verlor, verloren*
furious	*wütend*	lunchtime	*Mittagszeit*
get married	*heiraten*	mad	*verrückt*
gin	*Gin*	magician	*Zauberer*
Goodness me!	*Du meine Güte!*	married	*verheiratet*
grape	*Weintraube*	mask	*Maske*
greasy	*schmierig*	meat	*Fleisch*
greet	*grüßen*	medal	*Medaille*
grocer	*Lebensmittel-geschäft*	meeting	*Treffen*
		member	*Mitglied*
grow	*wachsen*	mess	*Unordnung*
guest	*Gast*	metal	*Metall*
handwriting	*Handschrift*	mine	*der meine, meinige*
have / has been	*gewesen sein*	mirror	*Spiegel*
headmaster	*Schuldirektor*	mistake	*Fehler*
healthy	*gesund*	mountain	*Berg*
help yourself	*bediene dich*	move	*übersiedeln*
hid	*versteckte*	napkin	*Serviette*
hide	*verstecken*	nasty	*schlimm*
hike	*wandern*	national anthem	*Landeshymne*
hiking tour	*Wanderung*	nearly	*fast, beinahe*
hit	*schlagen; Schlager*	nightmare	*Albtraum*
honest	*ehrlich*	nobody	*niemand*
hope	*Hoffnung, hoffen*	noodle	*Nudel*
hurt	*verletzt, verletzen*	north	*Norden*
husband	*Ehemann*	organize	*veranstalten*
instead	*anstatt*	other	*anderer*
iron	*bügeln*	pale	*blass*
Italian	*italienisch*	pancake	*Palatschinke*
Japanese	*japanisch*	parking space	*Parkplatz*
joke	*Witz*	parrot	*Papagei*
keep	*halten, behalten*	pass	*bestehen; vorbeigehen*
kite	*Papierdrachen*		
knit	*stricken*	pear	*Birne*
knock	*klopfen*	peel	*Schale (eines Obstes)*
language	*Sprache*	petrol station	*Tankstelle*
laugh	*lachen*	pick up	*abholen, aufheben*
lay	*etwas hinlegen*	planned	*geplant*
lazybone	*Faulpelz*	plate	*Teller*

Polish	polnisch	stable	Stall
pork	Schweinefleisch	step	steigen
prepare	zubereiten	stink	stinken
prison	Gefängnis	strike	schlagen, stoßen
prize	Gewinn	struck	schlug
promise	versprechen	stupid	dumm
proud of	stolz auf	such a	solch ein(-e,-es)
puddle	Pfütze	suitcase	Koffer
purse	Geldtasche	sunbathe	sonnenbaden
quarrel	Streit, streiten	sunshine	Sonnenschein
quite	ganz	supper	Abendessen
reach	erreichen	sweep	kehren, fegen
refuse	sich weigern	sweetheart	Liebling
repair	reparieren	tablecloth	Tischtuch
report	Zeugnis	take part in	teilnehmen an
resemble	ähnlich sein	take place	stattfinden
return	zurückgeben, -kehren	tale	Erzählung
ribbon	Band	taste	schmecken
riddle	Rätsel	tear	zerreißen
ride	Autofahrt; fahren	thrilling	spannend
run over (be)	überfahren werden	throat	Hals
salt shaker	Salzstreuer	tidy	aufräumen
save	sparen	tight	eng
scarf	Schal	till	bis
scream	Schrei; schreien	tore	zerriss
seaside (at the)	am Meer	travel	reisen
secret	Geheimnis	truth	Wahrheit
serve	servieren	Turkey	Türkei
set on fire	in Brand setzen	twice	zweimal
sew	nähen	tyre	Reifen
shave	rasieren	umbrella-stand	Schirmständer
size	Größe	unpleasant	unangenehm
skate	Eis- / Rollschuh laufen	veranda	Veranda
		victory	Sieg
sledge	Schlitten, (-fahren)	violence	Gewalt
slim	abnehmen; schlank	visitor	Besucher
slip	ausrutschen, entgleiten	war	Krieg
		weak	schwach
soft	weich	weep	weinen
solve	auflösen	well	gesund
sore	wund	wet	nass
soup	Suppe	wide	weit
Spain	Spanien	wooden	Holz-
sparkling wine	Sekt	youth	Jugend
spider	Spinne		
spill	verschütten		
spring	Frühling; springen		
sprinter	Läufer		
squirrel	Eichhörnchen		

KEY

page 1

went	hurt	brought
taught	wrote	felt
made	gave	caught
called	bit	crossed
thought	bought	ran
met	played	spent
cut	threw	dug
lost	sent	came
forgot	jumped	stayed
put	shut	said
took	read [*red*]	did
set	sang	paid
had	blew	began
visited	arrested	barked
watched	ho**pp**ed	saw
spoke	swam	pla**nn**ed
married	sto**pp**ed	studied
chose	arrived	found
drove	heard	broke
built	drew	drank
died	hurried	enjoyed
stank	fed	held
knew	let	opened
rang	worked	tried
stole	knocked	slept
ate	got	grew
hid	hit	shook
sold	shone	laughed
shot	won [*wʌn*]	wore
wept	told	stood
woke	left	fell
wanted	greeted	could
had to	was / were	turned
flew	became	cost
fought	froze	lent
hung	kept	laid
showed	sank	sprang
stroke	tore	fled

pages 2, 3

1. I always told / I didn't always tell
   What did I always tell my friends about?
2. He could come / He couldn't come
   When could he come?
3. I made; I didn't make / What did I make …?
4. We always played; We didn't always play
   When did we always play tennis?
5. She paid for; She didn't pay for
   Where did she pay for our dinner?
6. The children were good at skiing.
   … weren't good
   Who was good at skiing?
7. We bought
   We didn't buy **any** (☺ II / p19)
   What did we buy?
8. She tried; She didn't try
   Who did she try to catch?
9. The children made; didn't make
   Who made masks at school?
   Where did the children make masks?
10. I hoped to get;
    I didn't hope to get **any** (☺ II / p19)
    What did I hope to get?
11. They packed; They didn't pack
    What did they pack?
12. They acted out; They didn't act out
    What did they do at school?
13. We knew; We didn't know
    What did we know a lot about?
14. They went; They didn't go
    When did they go for a walk?
15. We cut out; We didn't cut out
    What did we cut out?
16. He put his arm; He didn't put his arm
    What did he put round her shoulders?
    Whose shoulders did he put his arm round?
17. I wanted; I didn't want
    What did I / you want?
18. We wrote; We didn't write
    Who did we write a lot of letters to?
19. Ann brought; didn't bring
    What did Ann bring to her mum?
20. Peter took; didn't take
    Where did Peter take the poster off?
21. We had; we didn't have
    When did we have breakfast in our holidays?
22. She cooked; didn't cook
    Who cooked for us? Who did she cook for?
23. We ate meat; We didn't eat
    When did we eat meat?
24. There was; There wasn't
    What was there in the grass?
25. We read; We didn't read
    What did we read?
26. He always did; He didn't always do
    What did he always do after school?
    When did he always do his homework?
27. We needed; We didn't need
    What did we need?
28. We looked; We didn't look at
    What did we look at?
29. He often bought; He didn't often buy
    Who did he often buy sweets for?
30. I had; I didn't have
    When did I / you have a party?
31. We went to see; We didn't go to see
    Who did we go to see?
32. He ran home to have lunch.
    He didn't run home to have lunch.
    Why did he run home?

33. He met; He didn't meet
    When did he meet her?
34. He laid the; He didn't lay
    Where did he lay the book?
35. We had to hurry. We didn't have to hurry.
    Who had to hurry?
36. Peter paid; didn't pay; What did Peter pay?
37. We knew; We didn't know
    Who did we know well?
38. She hid; didn't hide; Where did she hide?
39. He cut; He didn't cut; What did he cut?
40. He heard her. He didn't hear her.
    Who did he hear?
41. She said; didn't say; What did she say?
42. Mother sang; didn't sing
    What did mother sing?
43. The children ran; didn't run
    What did the children do?
44. We swam; We didn't swim
    Who swam in the lake?
45. He sat; He didn't sit; Where did he sit?
46. He told her; He didn't tell her
    Who told her everything?
    Who did he tell everything?
47. We spent; didn't spend
    Who spent a nice holiday?
48. Peter ate;
    didn't eat a lot of / **much** (☺ II / p87)
    What did Peter eat?
49. Frank gave; didn't give
    What did Frank give him?
    Who did Frank give the beer bottle?
50. Sandy could find; couldn't find
    What could Sandy find?
51. The plane left; didn't leave
    When did the plane leave?
52. He got; didn't get
    Who did he get a parcel from?
53. Susan wanted; didn't want; What did Susan want?
54. Alice took; didn't take; What did Alice take?
55. Her hair was; wasn't; What colour was her hair?
56. Ann stayed; didn't stay; Who did Ann stay with?
57. was; wasn't
    Where was my / your pullover from?
58. Sue read; didn't read
    What kind of book did Sue read?
59. Pit ran; didn't run because he wasn't late.
    Why did Pit run to the bus?
60. We visited; didn't visit
    When did we / you visit our / your granny?
61. was; wasn't
    How much was the new hat?
62. He got; didn't get
    Who did he get a letter from?
63. He offered; didn't offer her
    What did he offer her?
64. Tom went; didn't go
    Why did Tom go to market?
65. Bob took; didn't take
    Who did Bob take to town?
66. The Smiths came; didn't come
    When did the Smiths come?
67. Sarah liked; didn't like
    Who did Sarah like?

68. The children went; didn't go
    Where did the children go?
69. She looked; didn't look
    How did she look?
70. The ambulance took; didn't take
    Who did the ambulance take to hospital?
71. Bob was; wasn't
    Who was very tired?
72. Phil stayed; didn't stay
    Who did Phil stay in Vienna with?/
    Who did Phil stay with in Vienna?
73. The weather was; wasn't
    What was the weather like?
74. The Millers went; didn't go
    Who went to Italy? Where did the Millers go?
75. He always thought of; He didn't always think of
    Who did he always think of?
76. Our teacher gave;
    didn't give us a lot of / **much**   (☺ II / p87)
    Who gave us a lot of / **much** homework?
77. Our neighbours went; didn't go
    How did our neighbours go?
78. She wrote; didn't write
    Who did she write (to)?
79. Bill spent; didn't spend
    Where did Bill spend his holiday?

page 4

1. is drinking (Signalwort: *look*) (☺ I / p51,52)
2. drank (*yesterday*) (☺ I / p76,77)
3. played (*yesterday*)
4. is going to visit (*next*) (☺ I / p82)
5. is preparing (*now*) (☺ I / p51,52)
6. met (*ago*)
7. likes (generelle Aussage, pres.simple) (☺ I / p50)
8. were (*last*)
9. could not, was (*yesterday*)
10. was (*last week*)
11. are going to have (*next*) (☺ I / p82)
12. must do (*now*, keine ing-form bei *must*)
13. went, had (*last*)
14. bakes (*always*, generelle Aussage)
15. went, was (*ago*)
16. is (generelle Aussage, es ist immer dort) /
    was (wenn das Kino nicht mehr dort ist)
17. are you doing, I am posting
    (jetzt gerade) (☺ I / p51,52)
18. is going to meet (*tomorrow*), is,
    is jumping (*look*)
19. knocked, was (*yesterday*)
20. turned, ran, saw (*last*)
21. had to help (*yesterday*) (☺ II / p6,7)
22. must hurry (keine progressive form bei *must*)
    is waiting (jetzt gerade)
23. was, had to, missed, got,
    lost (*yesterday*) (☺ I / p76,77)

Schwierigkeiten bei dieser Übung?
Wiederholen: ☺ I / p50 (present simple)
               ☺ I / p51,52 (present progressive)
               ☺ I / p76,77 (past tense)

page 5

1. Excuse me, I am looking for the post office. Can you tell me, where it is?
2. Can you help me? I got lost. (I lost my way.)
3. I am a stranger, can you tell me the way to the opera?
4. I am a foreigner.
5. Is this the right way to the theatre?
6. Am I right for the station?
7. Excuse me, would you be so kind as to explain to me the way to the post office?
8. Is the post office next to the police station?
9. Cross the square and turn into the first street on the left (on your left) / and take the first left / and turn into the first left.
10. Go round the corner and you'll see the station at the end of / at the bottom of the street.
11. I'd like to eat something. Where is there a cheap restaurant?
12. Go straight ahead, turn right and there is a restaurant just opposite the station.
13. How long will it take me to walk to the station?
14. You can't miss the cinema. It is next to the chemist's.
15. You must turn left after the cinema. The hospital is opposite the big bridge.
16. You**'d better take** (you **had better take**) the second right (on your / on the right).
The phone box is in Park Road.
17. How long will the bus take to the station?
18. Am I right for the tourist information? / Is this the right way to the ...?
19. Go past the bridge. Don't cross it. / Don't go across it. Turn left at the traffic lights into Smith Road.
20. At the end / bottom of the square you'll see the bus stop.
21. You can't miss the supermarket. Go straight ahead and take the second left. Then go straight ahead again and turn left.
22. Go past the police station and take the third left after the hotel. You can't miss the zoo.
23. I'm going to ask the next passer-by where there is a baker.
24. Take the small road left (on your left) and you are standing (just) in front of the church.
25. May I ask you for the way to the opera?
26. Go down the road and wait at the bus stop.
27. Am I right for the hospital?

pages 8, 9, 10, 11

1. won't have to / will not have to
2. *Present tense*: don't have to / don't need to / haven't got to / needn't /
   Past tense: didn't have to / didn't need to
   Future: won't have to / won't need to
3. had to
4. were allowed to
5. won't have to / won't need to
6. must / have to; can; needn't / haven't got to / don't need to / don't have to
7. didn't have to / didn't need to
8. won't have to / won't need to
9. was not allowed to
10. Will you be allowed to
11. Were you allowed to
12. must / have to
13. *Present*: cannot / aren't able to; must / have to
    Past: couldn't / weren't able to; had to
    Future: won't be able to; will have to
14. Will he have to
15. was not allowed to
16. *Present*: needn't / don't have to / don't need to / haven't got to
    Past: didn't have to / didn't need to
    Future: won't have to / won't need to
17. will be allowed to (☺ II / p45,46)
18. *Present*: mustn't / aren't allowed to
    Future: won't be allowed to
19. will be able to (☺ II / p45,46)
20. didn't have to / didn't need to
21. will have to (☺ II / p45,46)
22. had to
23. will you have to
24. did you have to
25. had to
26. will have to; will have to;
    Present: needn't / don't have to / havent't got to / don't need to
    Future: won't have to
27. must / have to; mustn't / are not allowed to
28. *Present*: needn't / don't have to / don't need to / haven't got to
    Past: didn't have to / didn't need to
    Future: won't have to / won't need to
29. Could you / Were you able to; couldn't / was not able to / was unable to; didn't have to / didn't need to
30. won't have to (☺ II / p45,46)
31. *Present*: must / have to
    Future: will have to
32. *Present*: must / have to
    Future: will have to
33. mustn't / are not allowed to
34. could / was able to
35. could / was able to
36. *Present*: must / has to
    Past: had to
    Future: will have to
37. had to
38. *Present*: must / have to
    Future: will have to
39. wasn't allowed to
40. had to
41. *Present*: doesn't have to / doesn't need to / hasn't got to / needn't
    Future: won't have to
42. couldn't / wasn't able to / was unable to
43. *Present*: mustn't / aren't allowed to
    Past: weren't allowed to
    Future: won't be allowed to
44. *Present*: ca**nn**ot / isn't able to / is unable to
    Past: couldn't / wasn't able to / was unable to
    Future: won't be able to
45. *Present*: don't have to / don't need to / haven't got to / needn't
    Future: won't have to / won't need to
46. won't be able to / will be unable to

47. will be allowed to
48. *Present*: doesn't have to / doesn't need to / hasn't got to / needn't
    Past: didn't have to / didn't need to
    Future: won't have to / won't need to
49. couldn't / wasn't able to / was unable to
50. *Present*: must not / are not allowed to
    Past: weren't allowed to
    Future: won't be allowed to
51. *Present*: don't have to / don't need to / haven't got to / needn't
    Past: didn't have to / didn't need to
    Future: won't have to / won't need to
52. couldn't / wasn't able to / was unable to
53. didn't have to / didn't need to
54. could / was able to
55. didn't have to / didn't need to
56. *Present*: must / have to
    Past: had to
    Future: will have to
57. *Present*: don't have to / don't need to / haven't got to / needn't
    Future: won't have to / won't need to
58. could / were able to
59. will have to
60. could you / were you able to
61. was not allowed to
62. *Present*: must / have to
    Future: will have to
63. could he / was he able to
64. had to
65. mustn't / are not allowed to
66. don't have to / don't need to / haven't got to / needn't
67. couldn't / weren't able to / were unable to
68. could / was able to
69. didn't have to / didn't need to
70. won't be allowed to
71. couldn't / wasn't able to / was unable to
72. was allowed to
73. won't be able to
74. couldn't / weren't able to / were unable to
75. had to
76. *Present*: must not / are not allowed to
    Past: weren't allowed to
    Future: won't be allowed to
77. had to
78. *Present*: don't have to / don't need to / haven't got to / needn't
    Future: won't have to / won't need to
79. weren't allowed to
80. didn't have to / didn't need to
81. must not / are not allowed to
82. had to
83. *Present*: don't have to / don't need to / haven't got to / needn't
    Future: won't have to / won't need to
84. will be able to
85. could / was able to
86. *Present*: must / have to
    Future: will have to
87. was not allowed to
88. *Present*: don't have to / don't need to / haven't got to / needn't
    Future: won't have to / won't need to
89. had to
90. won't be able to
91. mustn't / are not allowed to
92. had to
93. will be able to
94. *Present*: don't have to / don't need to / haven't got to / needn't
    Past: didn't have to / didn't need to
    Future: won't have to / won't need to
95. had to; had to
96. mustn't / are not allowed to
97. won't be able to
98. didn't have to / didn't need to
99. will be able to
100. was not allowed to

pages 15, 16

1. I don't want / like / the blue dress.
   How about / What about / the green dress?
2. Let's hide! How about / What about / the garden?
3. I need a new notebook.
4. I'd like / I would like / new jeans.
5. Frank doesn't want to go / drive / to Linz.
6. He wants to go to bed now. I'm tired, too.
7. I've got new trousers. – How much **are they**?
8. I'd like to have some coffee now.
9. I don't need a babysitter!
10. **These** trousers **are** too long.
11. I need a new pen.
12. Do you like my picture?
13. Sandy would like (to have) a new game.
14. I want a new hat.
    I don't like the old hat any more.
15. She doesn't like / want / to go for a walk.
16. Does Peter come, too? – No, he is too small.
17. I'd like (to have) a slice / piece of cake, too.
18. We often play with her, too.
19. How / What / about the green trousers? –
    No, **they are** too long.
20. This exercise is too easy for us.
21. The specs / glasses / **are** too expensive.
22. I would like to come, but we go to Vienna.
23. He doesn't want / like / to sing.
    It's too boring for him.
24. My trousers **are** much / far / too tight.
25. I'd like / I would like / to help you.
26. I'd like / I would like / to ask you
    if you like / want / to come.
27. We go to the park to play / in order to play.
28. Listen to me!
29. I'd like to tell you something.
30. I want to tell you something.
31. I must / I have to / tell you something.
32. I need some help. How about / What about / you?
33. Let's bake a cake!
34. Would you like to play **with us**? – Yes, **I'd love to**!
35. He wants to go home now.
36. He'd like to go home now.
37. He doesn't want / like / to go home now.
38. I'd like to go to the cinema.
39. Could you tell me the way?
40. Let's go to town!

41. **I'd rather** go to Frank./ **I'd sooner** go to Frank!
42. How about / What about / a pizza?
43. These scissors don't work.
44. Would you please help me?
45. Come on! Let's help her!
46. Let's eat! I'm hungry!
47. I ought to be **with** Frank now / **at** Frank**'s** now.
48. You shouldn't laugh about her.
49. How about / What about / your new room?
50. I need two chairs.
51. Father wants to go into the bathroom now.
52. I'd like (to have) a cup of tea. / I'd love to have ...
53. Look at me!
54. You are too young to go to the party.
55. Thomas needs a new felt-tip.
56. Would you like to come with us?
57. Jenny wants (to have) a new umbrella.
58. He'd like to / would like to / buy a new desk.
59. The old table is too high.
60. He would like (to have) a new Ford, too.
61. You can't wear the jeans. **They are** too tight.
62. I'd like to go to Paris, too.
63. They hid Peter's school things, too.
64. I heard the doorbell, too.
65. He suddenly heard a noise, too.
66. Could you **take** me to town?
    Anmerkung:
    take bedeutet **vom Sprecher wegbringen**,
    bring bedeutet **zum Sprecher herbringen**.
67. Would you like to go to town with me?
68. The children need coloured pencils.
69. What colour is your dress? – It is blue, too.
70. The door was half-open, too.
71. Do you like cornflakes?
72. Would you like (to have) cornflakes now?
73. I hate meat, too.
74. Do you like the new book of Thomas Brezina?
75. How about / What about / a glass of milk?
76. He went home, too.
77. Susan needs a new school bag, too.
78. She couldn't believe her eyes:
    Tim wanted to kiss Mary!
79. He couldn't come. / He wasn't able to come. /
    He was unable to come.

page 17

1. during
2. during
3. during
4. While
5. during
6. during
7. during
8. during
9. during
10. While
11. while
12. while
13. during
14. while
15. during
16. during
17. during
18. during
19. During
20. while
21. during
22. while
23. during
24. during
25. while
26. during
27. during
28. While
29. during
30. during
31. while
32. during
33. during

pages 20, 21, 22, 23

1. some (Regel: some 1)
2. something (Regel: some 1)
3. any (Regel: any 1)
4. any (Regel: any 1)
5. any (Regel: any 1), anything (Regel: any 1)
6. anything / anybody / anyone (Regel: any 1)
7. anybody / anyone (Regel: any 3), any (Regel: any 3)
8. anything / anybody / anyone (Regel: any 3)
9. any (Regel: any 2)
10. anybody / anyone (Regel: any 2)
11. something (Regel: some 1)
12. some (Regel: some 2)
13. some (Regel: some 2)
14. something (Regel: some 1),
    somewhere (Regel: some 1)
15. somewhere (Regel: some 1)
16. any (Regel: any 4)
17. any (Regel: any 4)
18. any (Regel: any 4)
19. any (Regel: any 4)
20. any (Regel: any 4)
21. somebody / someone (Regel: some 1),
    some (Regel: some 1)
22. somebody / someone (Regel: some 2),
    somebody / someone / something (Regel: some 1)
23. anybody / anyone (Regel: any 3)
24. somebody / someone (Regel: some 1)
25. somebody / someone (Regel: some 1)
26. anything (Regel: any 1)
27. anybody / anyone (Regel: any 3)
28. something (Regel: some 2)
29. somewhere (Regel: some 2)
30. anything (Regel: any 1)
31. Someone / Somebody (Regel: some 1)
32. any (Regel: any 1), somewhere (Regel: some 1)
33. some (Regel: some 2)
34. somewhere (Regel: some 1)
35. something (Regel: some 1), anything (Regel: any 1)
36. some (Regel: some 1)
37. anybody / anyone (Regel: any 4)
38. some (Regel: some 2)
39. anywhere (Regel: any 4)

40. anybody / anyone (Regel: any 3),
    anything (Regel: any 3), anything (Regel: any 1)
41. anybody / anyone (Regel: any 3)
42. anything (Regel: any 4), anybody / anyone /
    anything (Regel: any 1)
43. any (Regel: any 4)
44. any (Regel: any 4), somewhere (Regel: some 1)
45. anything (Regel: any 1)
46. anybody / anyone / anything (Regel: any 1)
47. anywhere (Regel: any 1),
    somewhere (Regel: some 1)
48. some (Regel: some 1)
49. any (Regel: any 1)
50. any (Regel: any 1), some (Regel: some 1)
51. any (Regel: any 1)
52. anywhere (Regel: any 1),
    somewhere (Regel: some 1)
53. some (Regel: some 2), some (Regel: some 2)
54. some (Regel: some 2)
55. some (Regel: some 2), any (Regel: any 1)
56. some (Regel: some 2)
57. some (Regel: some 1), some (Regel: some 2)
58. some (Regel: some 1)
59. some (Regel: some 1)
60. any (Regel: any 1)
61. any (Regel: any 1)
62. some (Regel: some 2) or: any (Regel: any 2)
    je nachdem, welche Antwort ich erwarte
63. some (Regel: some 1)
64. anybody / anyone / anything (Regel: any 1)
65. somebody / someone (Regel: some 1)
66. some (Regel: some 2) or: any (Regel: any 2)
    je nachdem, welche Antwort ich erwarte
67. something (Regel: some 1), any (Regel: any 1),
    anywhere (Regel: any 1)
68. any (Regel: any 1), some (Regel: some 1)
69. something (Regel: some 1)
70. some (Regel: some 2)
71. any (Regel: any 1), some (Regel: some 1)
72. some (Regel: some 1)
73. something (Regel: some 2)
74. some (Regel: some 2) or: any (Regel: any 2)
    je nachdem, welche Antwort ich erwarte
75. some (Regel: some 1)
76. some (Regel: some 1)
77. any (Regel: any 1), some (Regel: some 1),
    any (Regel: any 4)
78. something (Regel: some 2), some (Regel: some 1)
79. something (Regel: some 1)
80. anything (Regel: any 1), some (Regel: some 1)
81. anything (Regel: any 1)
82. anybody / anyone / anything (Regel: any 1)
83. some (Regel: some 2)
    ich erwarte „ja", sonst würde ich nicht fragen
84. something (Regel: some 2), some (Regel: some 1)
85. any (Regel: any 1)
86. Some (Regel: some 1)
    Verneinung bezieht sich nur auf das Verb
87. anything (Regel: any 1), something (Regel: some 1)
88. somewhere (Regel: some 1)
89. some (Regel: some 2)
90. something (Regel: some 2), some (Regel: some 1)
91. something (Regel: some 1)
92. somewhere (Regel: some 1)
93. some (Regel: some 1)
94. something (Regel: some 1)
95. any (Regel: any 1)
96. some (Regel: some 1)
97. any (Regel: any 4)
98. Someone / somebody (Regel: some 1)
99. some (Regel: some 2), any (Regel: any 1)
100. anything (Regel: any 1)
101. anything (Regel: any 1)
102. somewhere (Regel: some 1)
103. Some (Regel: some 2)
104. any (Regel: any 1), some (Regel: some 1)
105. anybody / anyone (Regel: any 1)
106. any (Regel: any 4), any (Regel: any 4)
107. Some (Regel: some 1), anything (Regel: any 1)
108. anybody (Regel: any 1)
109. anybody / anyone (Regel: any 3),
     somewhere (Regel: some 1)
110. Any (Regel: any 4)
111. some (Regel: some 2)
112. anybody / anyone / anything (Regel: any 1)
113. Somebody / Someone (Regel: some 1)
114. somewhere (Regel: some 1),
     anywhere (Regel: any 1)
115. any (Regel: any 3)
116. somewhere (Regel: some 2)
117. Somebody / Someone (Regel: some 1)
118. some (Regel: some 2)
119. Somebody / Someone (Regel: some 1)
120. some (Regel: some 1), any (Regel: any 1)
121. Any (Regel: any 4)
122. anybody / anyone (Regel: any 2),
     anybody / anyone (Regel: any 2)
     ich erwarte, erhoffe die Antwort: nein
123. any (Regel: any 4) *nachdem ich nicht mehr
     sammle, kannst du alle, die du willst, nehmen.*
124. Any (Regel: any 4)
125. anything (Regel: any 2) or
     something (Regel: some 2)
     je nachdem, welche Antwort ich erwarte
126. any (Regel: any 2) or some (Regel: some 2)
     je nachdem, welche Antwort ich erwarte
127. anything (Regel: any 1)
128. any (Regel: any 1), any (Regel: any 1)
129. Someone / Somebody (Regel: some 1)
130. any (Regel: any 3)
131. anything (Regel: any 1)
132. any (Regel: any 1)

page 25

1. one
2. one
3. ones
4. ones
5. ones
6. ones (die Kleinen)
7. --- (Regel 1a)
8. --- (Regel 1a)
9. --- (Regel 4)
10. one; one
11. one
12. ones
13. --- (Regel 3)

14. one
15. ones
16. ones
17. --- (Regel 5)
18. --- (Regel 3)
19. --- (Regel 4)
20. one (Regel 1b)
21. --- (Regel 1a)
22. --- (Regel 2)
23. ones; ones
24. --- (Regel 3)
25. ones
26. one; one
27. one
28. one
29. --- (Regel 3)
30. one
31. one
32. ones
33. --- (Regel 4)
34. --- (Regel 5)
35. ones (*die Kleinen*) / one (*die Kleine, den Kleinen*)
36. --- (Regel 5)

pages 28, 29, 30

1. each, *jede Familie aus einer bestimmten Gruppe = in our town*
2. Each, *jeder Einzelne*
3. every, *steht bei important expressions*
4. every, *important expressions*
5. each, **of**, *an einzelnen bestimmten Tagen*
6. every
7. All, *all of a sudden = ganz plötzlich*
8. all, *mit Plural*
9. each, *auf jeder einzelnen Hausseite*
10. Every
11. Every
12. Each, *Signalwörter* **of, here**
13. Every, *mit Singular*
14. All, *mit Plural*
15. every
16. Each, *Signalwörter* **of, here**
17. all, *mit Plural*
18. Every, *mit Singular*
19. All, *mit Plural*
20. all, *mit Plural*
21. All, *mit Plural*
22. each, *(2 Hände)*
23. Each, *jede Einzelne der 2 Katzen*
24. Every
25. Each, *Signalwort* **of**
26. All, *mit Plural*
27. each, *(2 Seiten)*
28. each, *Signalwort* **of**
29. every, *every three hours = alle drei Stunden*
30. every, *every now and then = von Zeit zu Zeit*
31. Each, *Signalwort* **of**
32. All, *mit Plural (Merke: all the boys = all boys)*
33. every
34. each, *jedes einzelne Kind aus unserer Klasse*
35. All, *mit Plural (Merke: all the people = all people)*

36. Each, *Signalwort* **of** / or All = *alle*
37. All, *all that = alles was* / Everything
38. Each, *jeder einzelne Tourist des Hotels*
39. Every
40. every
41. all, *mit Plural*
42. each, *jedes einzelne Ticket*
43. each, *Signalwort* **of,** *für jeden einzelnen Wochentag*
44. all, *not at all = überhaupt nicht*
45. all, *all his money = sein ganzes Geld*
46. every
47. All, *mit Plural*
48. every, *every other day = jeden 2. Tag*
49. every
50. every
51. All, *mit Plural*
52. Everybody / Everyone, *mit Singular*
53. Each, *jedes einzelne Mädchen aus meiner Klasse*
54. everybody / everyone
55. Every
56. everything
57. all, *first of all = zu allererst,* everywhere
58. Everyone / Everybody, *mit Singular*
59. everyone / everybody, *mit Singular*
60. everyone / everybody
61. Every, *every time = jedesmal*
62. every, *every four weeks = alle vier Wochen*
63. All / Everything,
    all (that) = everything (that) = alles was
64. Every, *every time = jedesmal*
65. each, *Signalwort* **of**
66. Each, *Signalwort* **of,** *jeder Einzelne sagte so /*
    All, *alle sagten so*
67. Everybody / All
68. each, *an jeder einzelnen Straßenseite*
69. Every
70. all, *all day = den ganzen Tag*
71. every
72. Every
73. All, *mit Plural*
74. every
75. all, *all day = den ganzen Tag /*
    every, *every day = jeden Tag*
76. Each, **of**, *mit Singular*
77. all / everything (*all that = everything that = alles was*)
78. all, *all day = den ganzen Tag*
79. Everybody / Everyone
80. all, *all at once = ganz plötzlich*
81. All, *mit Plural*
82. Every
83. All, *mit Plural*
84. all
85. Each, *jeder Einzelne aus einer bestimmten Gruppe*
86. each, **of**
87. Each, **of**
88. All, *mit Plural*
89. Each, **of**, *mit Singular*
90. all, *mit Plural*
91. Every, *mit Singular*
92. All, *mit Plural*
93. all, *mit Plural*
94. all, *all together = alle gemeinsam*
95. Each, *jeder Einzelne aus einer bestimmten Gruppe*
96. Each

97. All, *mit Plural*
98. each
99. every, *every two hours = alle zwei Stunden*
100. every, *every now and then = hin und wieder, von Zeit zu Zeit*
101. everyday, *everyday clothes = Alltagsgewand*
102. every
103. All, *mit Plural*
104. every, *every two hours = alle zwei Stunden*
105. Each, **of** / All, *all of us = wir alle*
106. Each, *jedes einzelne Zimmer aus einer bestimmten Gruppe = aus diesem Hotel*
107. Each, *jeder einzelne Apfel aus dem Korb*
108. All, *mit Plural*
109. Each / All
110. each, *each other = einander*
111. every
112. each, *jedem Einzelnen gibt sie ...*
113. every, *every ten miles = alle zehn Meilen*
114. everywhere, each, *in jeder einzelnen Ecke*
115. all, *first of all = zu allererst,* everything
116. Each, *jeder von uns*
117. All, *mit Plural*

pages 31, 32

1. **As** (Regel 2)
2. **When** (Regel 2)
3. He is not **as** tall **as** I am. (Regel 3)
4. Tom Hanks plays **as** Forrest Gump. (Regel 5)
5. She is **as** clever **as** Pit. (Regel 3)
6. **When** will you come home? (Regel 1), **as** (Regel 4)
7. **As** you are so cheeky (Regel 2)
8. I don't know **when** he arrives. (Regel 1)
9. The Millers are **as** rich **as** the Smiths. (Regel 3)
10. **When** do you normally have breakfast? (Regel 1)
11. Since **when** have you (Regel 1)
12. nicer **as** she gets older. (Regel 1)
13. **As** a child he was (Regel 5)
14. **As** for you, you may leave. (Regel 6)
15. Till **when** can you stay? (Regel 1)
16. Leave everything **as** it is. (Regel 3)
17. **When** did that happen? (Regel 1)
18. Tell me **when** I can call. (Regel 1)
19. I did **as** he did (Regel 3) and now I work **as** a policeman. (Regel 5)
20. **When** were they at the airport? (Regel 1)
21. Do **as** you like! (Regel 3)
22. You may go **when** you are ready. (Regel 2)
23. **As** for me I must go now. (Regel 6)
24. **As** rich he is I won't marry him. (Regel 3) *wie reich er auch ist*
25. He did a lot of climbing **when** he was young. (Regel 2)
26. Would you be so kind **as** to close the window? (Regel 7)
27. He is twice **as** old **as** I. (Regel 3)
28. **When** he was in France he learned a lot. (Regel 2)
29. Madonna plays **as** Evita Peron. (Regel 5)
30. It was the same man **as** yesterday. (Regel 8)
31. He did **as** if I wasn't there. (Regel 4)
32. You treat me **as** a child. (Regel 3)
33. Call **whenever** you want to. (Regel 3)
34. **As** you yourself said, it is too late now. (Regel 3)
35. It was raining **when** we arrived. (Regel 2)
36. **When** do you want (Regel 1)
37. **when** (Regel 2)
38. **When** she is away (Regel 2) / **As** (Regel 2) / **Whenever** (Regel 3)
39. **as** much **as** (Regel 3)
40. same age **as** I (Regel 8)
41. **as** much **as** (Regel 3)
42. **when** he comes (Regel 2) / **as soon as** (Regel 9)
43. **As** the school year (Regel 2) / **When** (Regel 2)
44. **When** you go away (Regel 2)
45. **When** I get up (Regel 2)
46. **as** many friends **as** (Regel 3)
47. **as** fast **as** you (Regel 3)
48. **When** (Regel 2) / **As soon as** (Regel 9) / **As** (Regel 2)
49. **as** old **as** (Regel 3)
50. the same colour **as** (Regel 8)
51. **as** much **as** you do (Regel 3)
52. **As** they live (Regel 2)
53. just **as** Ben wanted to go (Regel 11)
54. **as** father tells you (Regel 3)
55. the same drink **as** yesterday (Regel 8)
56. **as** long **as** (Regel 10)
57. at five **as** well (Regel 12)
58. **As** an Austrian (Regel 5)

pages 40, 41, 42, 43

1. fast, faster
2. interesting, most interesting
3. good, better
4. prettiest, prettier
5. nice, nicer
6. many, more
7. more expensive, expensive
8. bad, worse
9. heavier, heaviest
10. most beautiful, more beautiful
11. beautiful, more beautiful
12. cheaper
13. more expensive
14. fast
15. more comfortable
16. cheap, cheaper
17. big, bi**gg**er
18. little, less (*unzählbar*)
19. small / little, smallest
20. many, more, most (*zählbar*)
21. few, fewer (*zählbar*)
22. good, better
23. bad, worse
24. heavy, heav**i**er, heav**i**est
25. more difficult, most difficult
26. younger, younger / youngest
27. elder, older
28. oldest
29. good, better, best
30. bad, worse
31. worse, worst
32. farther, farther, farthest
33. nearest, next

34. nearest (*am nächsten gelegen*) / next (*in der Reihenfolge*)
35. last
36. latest
37. latest
38. last
39. farther, farthest
40. nearest (*am nächsten gelegen*)
41. busy, busier / dilligent, more dilligent
42. **fu**rther
43. **e**lder / **e**ldest, older
44. nearest (*am nächsten gelegen*), next (*in der Reihenfolge*)
45. less, better
46. bad, worst / wicked, most wicked
47. best
48. careful, more careful
49. bad, worse
50. fat, fa**tt**er, fa**tt**est
51. careful, more careful, most careful
52. good, cleverest
53. nearest (*am nächsten gelegen*), next (*in der Reihenfolge*)
54. next, last
55. **fu**rther
56. later
57. last
58. nearest
59. next
60. farther / further
61. last, last
62. farther / further
63. fewer, fewest (*zählbar*)
64. better / healthier (*gesünder*)
65. most interesting
66. more doubtful
67. last
68. last
69. more expensive
70. heav**i**er
71. thi**nn**est
72. bad, worse
73. last, more expensive
74. handsomest
75. worse
76. best
77. **fu**rther
78. wind**i**er
79. most wicked / worst
80. severer / stricter
81. more comfortable, fewer (*zählbar*), less (*unzählbar*)
82. drier
83. bi**gg**est
84. more thrilling
85. more exciting
86. fewer (*zählbar*)
87. less (*unzählbar*), least
88. most beautiful / pre**tti**est
89. smaller
90. most elegant
91. nearest (*am nächsten gelegen*)
92. little (*unzählbar*), more
93. not so expensive as / not as expensive as

page 44

1. as nervous as
2. faster than / quicker than
3. less than
4. much better than / far better than
5. much / far / younger than
6. a bit higher than
7. not so expensive as / not as expensive as
8. the same time as
9. less than
10. much / far / ho**tt**er than
11. a bit more tired than
12. not so far as / not as far as
13. the same colour as
14. much more time than / far more ...
15. much less time than / far less ...
    (*little – less – least für unzählbare Ausdrücke*)
16. much fewer badges than
    (*few – fewer – fewest für zählbare Ausdrücke*)
17. less than
18. much sa**dd**er than / far sa**dd**er than
19. not so / not as / expensive as
20. much less than / far less than
21. much fewer stamps than
22. the same car as
23. a bit cleverer than / a bit smarter than
24. much taller than / far taller than
25. much fewer problems than (*zählbar, Plural*)
26. not so difficult as / not as difficult as
27. less than
28. less pleasant than
29. much fewer mistakes than / far fewer ...
30. much **more fun** than
31. as difficult as
32. not so confused as / not as confused as
33. much more wine than

pages 48, 49, 50, 51

Anmerkung: statt *will* kann immer die Kurzform *'ll* verwendet werden!

1. will / 'll (*worry*), will / 'll (*think*) (Regel A)
2. is going to (D)
3. is going to (A)
4. will / 'll (*hope*) (A)
5. will / 'll (A)
6. will (A)
7. will (A)
8. are you going to (A)
9. will (A)
10. will (A)
11. will not / won't (A)
12. will (A)
13. will (A)
14. are you going to (A), will (A)
15. will (B)
16. won't (A)
17. will (B)
18. won't (A)
19. will (A)

20. will (A)
21. is going to (B)
22. will (A)
23. am going to (B)
24. will (A)
25. will (A)
26. am going to (A/C) / will (C)
27. will (A)
28. will (B)
29. will (A)
30. Are you going to (A) / will (C)
31. will (A), won't (A)
32. won't (B)
33. will (A)
34. will (A)
35. Are you going to (A/C)
36. will, will (A)
37. will (B)
38. is not going to (D)
39. will (B)
40. is he going to (A)
41. will (C)
42. am going to (A/C), will (A)
43. will (B)
44. will (*think*) (C)
45. is going to (A/C)
46. won't (A)
47. are you going to (A), will (*think*) (C)
48. won't, will (B)
49. am going to (A/C)
50. ll (C)
51. Are you going (☺ I p 82, Merke)
52. Is she going (☺ I p 82, Merke)
53. will (C) s*pontaner Entschluss im Moment des Sprechens, das Rad sofort zu reparieren. Vergleiche dazu Satz 95*
54. will (A)
55. will (A), will (C) *spontaner Entschluss im Moment des Sprechens, die grüne Bluse anzuprobieren.*
56. will (A)
57. is going to (B/D)
58. will (A), are going to (A/C)
59. will (C)
60. will (A)
61. won't (A)
62. is going to (A)
63. is going to (A)
64. is going to (A)
65. are going to (A)
66. are going to (A), will (A) (*Befürchtung*)
67. will (A)
68. will (A) (*Befürchtung, Vermutung*)
69. is going to (A/C)
70. will (A)
71. am going to (C) *or* will (C) *entweder eine bereits vorher getroffene Entscheidung oder ein spontaner Entschluss während des Sprechens*
72. won't (C)
73. are going to (A/C), is going to (B) *or* will (A)
74. is going to (A)
75. will (C)
76. Is she going (☺ I p 82, Merke), won't (*think*) (A)
77. is going to (D)
78. isn't going to (D/B) / won't (A)

79. will (B)
80. won't (B)
81. will (A)
82. won't (A)
83. will (C)
84. won't (A)
85. will (A)
86. will (B)
87. will (A)
88. will (A)
89. will (C)
90. are you going to (A)
91. will (A)
92. will (A)
93. will (A)
94. will (A)
95. am going to (C) *kein spontaner Entschluss, das Rad zu reparieren. Er wusste bereits gestern davon. Vergleiche Satz 53*
96. am going to (A/C)
97. will you (A) *Hoffnung, Erwartung*
98. will (B), *er kann die Prüfungen persönlich nicht beeinflussen*
99. Will you (E)
100. am going to (A/C) *or* will (C)
101. Will Bob (A)
102. will (A/C)
103. am going to (A)
104. is going to (D)
105. will (A)
106. Will she (A) / Is she going to (A/C)
107. isn't going to (B/A)
108. is going to (D)
109. am going to (C/A)
110. is going to (D)
111. will (A)
112. are going to (A)
113. is going to (A)
114. will (A) *unsichere Vorhersage*
115. will (A)
116. is not going to (D)
117. will (A)
118. are you going to (A)
119. are going to (A)
120. will (A)
121. will (A)
122. will (A)
123. will (A)
124. is going to (B)
125. are going to (B)
126. will (B)
127. won't (A)
128. will (A)
129. will (A)
130. will (C)
131. will (A)
132. will (D)
133. Will you (E)
134. will (B) *er kann es persönlich nicht ändern, dass er 40 wird*, are going to have (A)
135. will (A), am going to (A/C)
136. will (C)
137. will (A)
138. will (B)

139. will (B)
140. will (D)
141. Will you (E)
142. will (C)
143. won't (A) *Hoffnung, Erwartung*

pages 55, 56, 57

1. heavily
2. easily
3. clever
4. angrily
5. slowly
6. early
7. slowly
8. quietly
9. quietly
10. difficult
11. clearly, slowly
12. well
13. perfectly
14. perfect
15. bad
16. fast / quickly
17. quiet, carefully
18. well
19. good, well
20. fair, good
21. fair, well
22. cheap
23. sad
24. happily
25. daily
26. quickly, carefully
27. good, well
28. well
29. beautifully, beautiful
30. fast, good
31. angrily
32. badly
33. carefully, long, easily
34. politely, polite
35. badly
36. carelessly
37. fair
38. late
39. near, dangerous
40. hard, good
41. well
42. busy
43. quickly, strong
44. heavily, full
45. badly, quickly, fast
46. nervous, carefully
47. busily, tired, quickly
48. beautifully
49. clearly
50. hard, badly
51. happily, lovely
52. loudly, well
53. well, good
54. happily, beautifully
55. fantastically

56. late
57. early, high
58. well, quickly
59. high
60. quickly
61. proudly
62. sadly
63. well
64. wonderfully
65. good, well
66. quickly
67. loudly
68. luckily, high
69. quickly, hungry
70. cold, quickly
71. easily, famous
72. absolutely
73. high
74. deeply
75. perfectly
76. quietly, sadly
77. prettily
78. fast
79. honestly
80. nicely
81. possibly
82. daily
83. straight
84. early
85. dangerously, fast
86. high
87. monthly
88. quickly

page 61

1. for
2. back
3. at
4. over
5. out, up
6. —
7. on, alone
8. into
9. about
10. up
11. in
12. out
13. in / up
14. across, round
15. back
16. out
17. out
18. off
19. back
20. into
21. down on
22. through
23. to
24. for
25. back, up
26. after
27. out

28. out
29. up
30. out
31. forward to
32. to
33. out
34. in
35. down

page 62

1. helped
2. would be
3. would cry
4. would he do
5. would be
6. saw
7. would Laura do
8. came
9. would buy
10. would you do
11. would do
12. lost
13. would be
14. missed
15. would you do
16. would be
17. would you do
18. would be
19. watched
20. could
21. would you answer
22. forgot
23. were
24. saw

pages 66, 67

Mehrere Lösungen sind möglich. Hier einige Vorschläge:

1. **While** I am waiting for the doctor I am reading a book.
2. I bought a bottle of sparkling wine, **but** I didn't drink it. / **Although / Even though / Though** I bought a bottle of sparkling wine, I didn't drink it.
3. Did Milly go out last night **or** did she stay at home?
4. Should we walk **or** should we call a taxi?
5. I must shut the window **because** it is too windy. / **As / Since** it is too windy, I must shut ...
6. It was cold, **so / that's why / therefore** we didn't go swimming. / We didn't go swimming **because** it was cold. / **As / Since** it was cold, we didn't go swimming.
7. **Before** you answer the question, think carefully.
8. **If** you don't run you won't catch the bus.
9. What's the name of the river **that / which** flows through Linz?
10. Yesterday I saw a woman on TV **who** could speak ...
11. Linda is wearing a shirt **which / that** is far too long for her.
12. **When** Mrs Miller came in she was pale in the face.
13. Liz wants to have **both** new jeans **and** a new pullover. / Liz **not only** wants to have new jeans, **but also** a new pullover.
14. **Neither** Tom **nor** Nick likes popcorn.
15. You can have a sandwich **or** toast. / You can have **either** a sandwich **or** toast. / You can have **both** a sandwich **and** toast.
16. Tony wanted to carry his bike, **but** he was too weak.
17. Stella was tired **and** went to bed. / **As / Since** Stella was tired, she went to bed. Stella was tired, **that's why** she went to bed. / Stella was tired, **so** she went to bed.
18. My summer coat was expensive, **but** my winter coat was even more expensive.
19. The exam was not easy, **but** Bob was able to pass it. **Although / Though / Even though** the exam was not easy, Bob was able to pass it.
20. Eve studied a lot **in order to** get a good report. Eve studied a lot **to** get a good report. / Eve wanted to get a good report, **that's why** she studied a lot. / **As / Since** Eve wanted to get a good report, she studied a lot.
21. Pamela is short and slim, **whereas** her brother is tall and fat. / Pamela is short and slim, **but** her brother ...
22. **Neither** Nora **nor** Lynn can go to Pit's party.
23. I can't buy a new car **because** I haven't got any money. / I haven't got any money, **that's why** I can't buy a new car. / **As / Since** I haven't got any money, I can't buy a new car. / I haven't got any money, **so** I can't buy a new car.
24. **Although / Though / Even though** it was rainy and stormy, they went for a walk. / It was rainy and stormy; **nevertheless,** they went for a walk. / It was rainy and stormy, **but** they went for a walk.
25. I feel tired **because** I didn't sleep much last night. / I didn't sleep much last night, **that's why** I feel tired. / **As / Since** I didn't sleep much, I feel tired.
26. Roger left home at five **in order to** catch the six o'clock train. / Roger left home at five **to** catch ... / Roger left home at five **because** he wanted to catch ... / Roger wanted to catch the six o'clock train; **therefore / that's why** he left home at five.
27. We can go **either** to the Greek restaurant **or** to the Italian restaurant.
28. Her new friend is **not only** very charming **but** nice and polite **as well**. / Her new friend is **not only** very charming **but also** nice and polite.
29. I wanted to bake a cake, **but** there wasn't any flour left. / I wanted to bake a cake, **however**; there wasn't any flour left.
30. We can buy **either** a book **or** flowers for her. / We can buy **both** a book **and** flowers for her. / We can buy a book **and** flowers for her. / We can buy **not only** a book **but also** flowers for her.
31. She was very nasty to him, **but** he loves her. / **Although / Though / Even though** she was very nasty to him, he loves her. / She was very nasty to him; **nevertheless**, he loves her.
32. **If** you don't study harder you won't pass the exam. / Study harder **or** you won't pass the exam.
33. This is the black dog **that / which** bit Sandra yesterday.
34. She doesn't eat much **because** she wants to slim. / **As / Since** she wants to slim, she doesn't eat much. / She wants to slim **that's why** she doesn't eat much.

35. She has got a headache, **that's why** she is going to bed. / **As / Since** she has got a headache, she is going to bed. / She is going to bed **because** she has got a headache.
36. **As / Since** she is very nice, everybody likes her. / She is very nice **so** everybody likes her. / She is very nice, **that's why** everybody likes her.
37. **After** the very big meal, I was tired.
38. I helped him so much; **nevertheless,** he was very unfriendly to me. / I helped him so much, he, **however**, was very unfriendly to me. / **Even though** I helped him so much, he was ...
39. We can spend our holidays **either** in Greece **or** in Turkey.
40. You may go out now, **but** don't be late for dinner. **If** you aren't late for dinner you may go out now.
41. I don't like **either** pork **or** beef. / I like **neither** pork **nor** beef.
42. **Before** you jump into the pond (you must) see if it's deep enough.
43. She studies hard / **in order to** / **to** pass her ... / She wants to pass her driving licence, **that's why** she studies hard. / She studies hard **because** she wants to ...
44. **Since / As** it's too late, we can't visit him. / We can't visit him **because** it's too late.
45. I bought a new dress, **but** it's too tight. / I bought a new dress **that / which** is too tight.
46. She is **not only** a very good mother **but** a very good cook **as well**. / She is **both** a very good mother **and** a very good cook. / She is a very good mother **and** a very good cook.
47. Will you come at eight **or** (at) nine? / **When** will you come, at eight **or** nine?
48. She looks after her flowers every day, **that's why** she has got nice flowers in her garden. / She has got nice flowers ... **and** looks after them every day. / **Since / As** she looks after her flowers every day, she has got nice flowers in ...
49. Mother is preparing dinner **while** the ...
50. **Even though / Although / Though** it was very late, he called her. / It was very late, **nevertheless / but** he called her.
51. This is Mr Funny, **who** has got a pink car.
52. Milly likes spinach, **whereas** Bob doesn't like it. / Milly likes spinach, **but** Bob doesn't like it.
53. **Even though / Although / Though** he is very poor, he is very happy. / He is very poor; **nevertheless,** he is very happy. / He is very poor, **but** he is ...
54. Jim is angry **because** he can't find ... / Jim can't find his purse, **that's why** he is angry. / **As / Since** Jim can't find his purse, he is angry.
55. Sally wanted to be alone, **that's why** she went up a mountain. / Sally went up a mountain **because** she wanted to be alone. / Sally went up a mountain **in order to** be alone. / ... **to** be alone.
56. I had no dinner, **that's why** I woke up and was hungry. / **As / Since** I had no dinner, I woke up and was hungry.
57. **After** a long ride Tom was tired. / Tom had a long ride, **that's why** he was tired.
58. **As / Since** she is very nice to him, he loves her. / She is very nice to him, **that's why** he loves her.
59. I want **neither** a new dress **nor** a new hat.
60. He hurried **because** he wanted to meet her at the airport. / He wanted to meet her at the airport, **that's why** he hurried. / **Since / As** he wanted to meet her at the airport, he hurried.
61. His girlfriend left him, **that's why** he is so sad. / He is so sad **because** his girlfriend left him.
62. Eve is nice and charming, **whereas** her sister is arrogant and unfriendly.
63. **Neither** we **nor** our neighbours saw the accident.
64. She got a nice birthday present, **that's why** she is so happy. / **Since / As** she got a nice birthday present, she is so happy. / She is so happy **because** she got a nice birthday present.
65. **As / Since** Nick is older than his brother, he stays up late. / Nick is older than his brother, **that's why** he stays up late. / Nick is older than his brother, **so** he stays up late.
66. Peter has to study for his exam, **that's why** he must stay at home. / **As / Since** Peter has to study for his exam, he must stay at home. / Peter must stay at home **because** he has to study for his exam. / Peter must stay at home **in order to / to** study for...
67. I don't like Charlie **because** he isn't very nice. / **As / Since** Charlie isn't very nice, I don't like him. / Charlie isn't very nice, **that's why** I don't like him.
68. We can invite her **either** for dinner **or** for lunch. / We can invite her **both** for dinner **and** for lunch. / We can invite her **not only** for dinner **but** for lunch **as well**.
69. You can have **either** a lemonade **or** a Coke. / You can have **both** a lemonade **and** a Coke.
70. **As / Since** the exam was very difficult, Lisa failed. / The exam was very difficult, **that's why** Lisa failed. / Lisa failed **because** the exam was very difficult.
71. **Before** you go to bed, brush your teeth / Brush your teeth **before** you go to bed. / Brush your teeth **(and) then** go to bed.
72. He broke the window, **but** his mother wasn't angry with him. / **Even though / Though / Although** he broke the window, his mother wasn't angry with him. / He broke the window, his mother, **however**, wasn't angry with him.
73. This is Mrs Chatterbox, **who** knows everything about everybody.
74. Don't tell her anything **because** she can't keep a secret. / **Since / As** she can't keep a secret, don't tell her anything.
75. **Before** an exam I can't eat anything. / **After** an exam I can't eat anything. / **When** I've got an exam I can't eat anything. / I've got an exam, **that's why** I can't eat anything.
76. This is the new bag **that / which** I bought yesterday.
77. You are happy **because** you don't make many mistakes. / **As / Since** you don't make many mistakes, you are happy.

page 72

1. since 2016
2. for many years
3. for 15 years
4. since her youth
5. for three weeks
6. since Christmas
7. since my last holidays
8. For how long
9. since last Friday
10. for three hours
11. for eight years
12. since 2017
13. for two weeks
14. since Friday, for eight days
15. for a month
16. since Easter
17. for two hours
18. since January
19. for more than two months
20. for ages
21. for many weeks
22. since last year
23. for more than a month
24. since breakfast
25. since this morning
26. since their quarrel
27. Since when
28. for a long time
29. for a month
30. for two years
31. since the beginning of the year
32. for more than four weeks
33. since lunchtime
34. since 2015
35. For how long
36. (for) very long
37. since January
38. since her youth

pages 73, 74, 75, 76, 77

1. went (*Signalwort: last*) (☺ I / p76,77)
2. drove (*fünf mal fuhr er, das ist vorbei, kein Bezug zur Gegenwart*)
3. Have you met (*hast du sie heuer schon getroffen?*)
4. studied (*als sie in der Schule war, das ist vorbei*)
5. have lived (*Signalwort for, sie leben noch immer dort*)
6. was (*last*, ☺ I p76,77)
7. lived (*from ... to*, ☺ I p76,77)
8. has been (*since*)
9. saw (*ago*)
10. worked (*last*)
11. have never seen (*never*)
12. Have you seen (*Bezug zur Gegenwart, die Schlüssel sind nicht da*)
13. left (*last*)
14. cried (4-mal, vorbei)
15. Have you met him yet? (*Signalwort yet*)
16. had to (*the week before last*)
17. went (*diese 2-mal sind vorbei*)
18. Have you seen (*schon gesehen*)
19. had to, missed (*yesterday*)
20. finished (*ago*)
21. read (*ago*)
22. has not arrived yet / has not yet arrived (*yet*)
23. has just switched on (*just*)
24. gave up (*last*)
25. had (*ago*)
26. was (*last*), have not seen (*since*)
27. Have you been (*yet*)
28. went, met (*when*)
29. bought (*last*)
30. have not visited (*since*)
31. have not been (*for*)
32. did you write (*when*), wrote (*last*)
33. met (*ago*)
34. have just had (*just*)
35. has not drunk (*for*)
36. Have you read (*yet*), have not read (*not yet*), read (*last*), liked
37. Have you ever been (*ever*)
38. have not played (*for*)
39. spent (*last*)
40. have you had (*Wie lange hast du ihn schon?*), bought (*last*), have had (*for*)
41. have just brought (*just*)
42. has he been (*since*), came (*yesterday*)
43. have never been (*never*)
44. Did you sleep (*last*)
45. have not seen (*not yet*)
46. has she been (*ist sie schon krank*)
47. was (*last year*) (*for* heißt hier nicht: *seit!*)
48. did you have (*Frühstück war um acht – vorbei*)
49. have not had (*since*)
50. Have you ever been (*ever*), was (*in the summer of 2017*)
51. I have lost, Have you seen (*Bezug zur Gegenwart: die Schlüssel sind verschwunden*)
52. did you spend (*in 2016* – Ferien sind vorbei)
53. went (*yesterday*), has had (*since*)
54. have you read (*hast du es schon gelesen?*), read (*during the holidays* – vorbei)
55. did you arrive (*ago*)
56. have not played (*since*)
57. finished (*ago*)
58. did you see (*last*)
59. has washed (*It is wet now* – Bezug zur Gegenwart, Resultat vorhanden)
60. posted (*yesterday*)
61. has not seen (*not yet*)
62. has *already* tried on
63. has worked (*since*)
64. was (*from ... to*)
65. listened (*yesterday*)
66. Have you met (*lately*), have not met (*since*)
67. have worked (*Resultat: die fertige Arbeit*)
68. worked (*ago*)
69. had (*last*)
70. went (*in 2017*)
71. has not been (*since*)
72. have not arrived (*not yet*)
73. did you not answer, called (*at eight*, vorbei)
74. have not had (*for*)
75. did you wake up (*when*)
76. have played (*Resultat: They are dirty now.*)

77. have just woken up (*just*)
78. swept (*ago*), have done (Resultat: *It's dirty again.*)
79. has been (*for*)
80. hurt (*last*), has hated (*since*)
81. has gone (Resultat: *he isn't here*)
82. has rained (Resultat: *the streets are wet*)
83. has *never* been
84. went (*when he was fourteen*, vorbei)
85. have *never* learned / learnt; learned or learnt (*when he was six*, vorbei)
86. has *already* baked
87. has happened (Resultat: *you are bleeding*)
88. Have you drunk (*yet*), has been (Resultat: *er ist noch immer zu heiß*)
89. Has the baker brought the bread *yet*?, hasn't (Resultat: *das Brot ist noch immer nicht da*)
90. returned (*ago*)
91. moved (*last*)
92. took (*ago*)
93. Were your parents, weren't (*last*)
94. Have you seen (*lately*), have not met (*since*)
95. have not been (*since*), was (*four years,* vorbei)
96. has not been (*for*)
97. went (*ago*)
98. Did she borrow (*last*), hasn't yet returned (*yet* könnte auch am Satzende stehen)
99. have not had (*since*), left (*in 2010*, vorbei)
100. have they lived (*for* 5 years), bought, was (*when*, vorbei)
101. Have you *ever* seen, went, was (*when*)
102. Have you had (*since*), arrived (*yesterday*), have not yet talked (*since*), came (ich kam gestern)
103. Did it rain (er ist nicht mehr in Cornwall), was, did you come (*yesterday*)
104. have been (*since*), have been (sie sind noch immer dort)
105. have you had (*for*)
106. have done, have spilt / spilled (Resultat: das schmutzige T-Shirt)
107. forgot (*last*)
108. have worked (Resultat: awfully tired)
109. have understood (since), explained (Sie erklärte die Regeln *damals*, seither verstehe ich sie)
110. has been (Es ist mir *schon seit Beginn* klar.)
111. have not had (*since*), talked (*last*)
112. has not finished (*not yet*)
113. did (*ago*)
114. did he come (*when*), arrived (*at six*, vorbei)
115. has never seen (*up to now*)
116. did you drink (*last*)
117. has *just* left
118. was (*yesterday*)
119. Did you wear, were, wore (*when he was at school*, vorbei)
120. broke (*in June*, vorbei), has not been able to (*since*) ☺ II / p89
121. has *not yet* arrived / has*n't* arrived yet
122. have not seen (*for*)
123. have *just* arrived
124. did you meet (damals, vorbei)
125. started (*in 2015*), has been (*up to now*)
126. Have you *ever* eaten, ate (*last*)
127. bought (*last*)
128. left (*ago*), started (damals)
129. has *never* seen (*a* UFO, ☺ I / p1: Attention)
130. saw (*before*)
131. Have they *ever* given, gave (*last*)
132. have not watched (*this* week, noch nicht vorbei)
133. saw (*last*)
134. Have you been (*this*), was (*last*)
135. have you had (*today*, noch nicht vorbei), felt, had (*yesterday*)
136. has Sarah been (*since*), arrived (*on Friday,* vorbei), has been (*for*)
137. has not smoked (*for*)
138. has washed (Resultat: *they are clean now*)
139. was (*on Tuesday*, vorbei)

page 78

1. his
2. theirs
3. ours
4. its / his / hers
5. mine
6. his
7. Mine, hers
8. Ours
9. Mine
10. His
11. yours
12. mine
13. Ours
14. **of** theirs

pages 80, 81, 82, 83, 84, 85, 86

1. wasn't (von *be* ist keine progressive form möglich), was playing (Regel 1)
2. wasn't watching (wenn ich Dauer betonen will) / didn't watch, was reading (1)
3. were you doing, was having (4)
4. did he say (es soll hier nicht die Dauer betont werden), wasn't listening (1)
5. was raining (1), didn't go (es soll hier nicht die Dauer betont werden)
6. was working (1/4)
7. woke up, was shining (3)
8. was still working (4)
9. were having (2), was (von *be* ist keine progressive form möglich)
10. were you doing, was having (4)
11. was, was watching (1)
12. was watching, rang (3)
13. was driving (4)
14. was (keine progressive form bei *be*), was waiting (4)
15. were taking (4)
16. was washing (4)
17. was having (4)
18. couldn't (keine progressive form bei *can*), was crying (1)
19. was Tom doing, met (3), was shopping (1)
20. was Tina wearing (1) (Dauer soll betont werden) / did Tina wear (Dauer soll nicht betont werden)
21. was it raining, were taking (2)

22. was reading, was knitting (2)
23. was he doing, went, was trying (3)
24. saw, was carrying (3)
25. saw, was wearing, was carrying (3)
26. was (keine progressive form bei *be*), was smoking (2)
27. was John doing, rang (3), was hanging up (2)
28. were you watching, called (3), was crying (2)
29. started, stopped (zwei Folgehandlungen, keine Gleichzeitigkeit)
30. went (als wir gerade losgehen wollten, neu eintretende Handung), / were going (als wir bereits unterwegs waren), was snowing (1/2)
31. saw, were waiting (1)
32. fell, was reading (3)
33. was counting, came (3)
34. was walking, met (3)
35. were sitting, started (3)
36. were having, broke (3)
37. was hanging up, fell (3)
38. broke, slipped (zwei schnelle Ereignisse)
39. wasn't, left (Folgehandlung: und so ging er ...)
40. wasn't, went (Dauer der Handlung unwichtig)
41. got up, brushed, combed, had (lauter Folgehandlungen)
42. brought, were having (3)
43. met (kurzes Ereignis), was wearing (1)
44. was reading, was waiting (2)
45. fell out (schnelle Handlung), was having (3)
46. was having, was watching (2)
47. stole, did you see (Dauer der Handlung unwichtig)
48. broke (schnell), were playing (3)
49. was waiting, returned (3)
50. fell, was running (3)
51. got up, was, took (lauter Folgehandlungen)
52. wasn't driving, happened (3)
53. didn't go, was, had (Dauer unwichtig) / was having (Dauer wichtig)
54. were you doing (4)
55. lost, was running (3)
56. was doing, was trying (2)
57. Was she wearing, saw (3)
58. went, saw (zwei Folgehandlungen), was baking (sie war bereits beim Backen: 3)
59. opened, was waiting (3)
60. were walking, were singing (2)
61. were talking about, didn't hear (*hear* steht normalerweise nicht in der progressive form)
62. was looking, was playing (2)
63. saw, smiled (zwei Folgehandlungen: zuerst sah er sie, dann lächelte er)
64. was listening, began (3)
65. were sitting, heard (3)
66. were travelling, met (3)
67. was riding, got (3)
68. was washing, was feeding (2)
69. was washing, came (3)
70. were looking out, was snowing (2)
71. were having, brought (3)
72. was hiding, were talking (2)
73. didn't hear (*hear* steht normalerweise nicht in der progressive form), were playing (1)
74. was he doing, was cutting (4)
75. were sitting, broke (3)
76. was having, rang (3)
77. phoned (4 mal, Folgehandlungen), were you (keine progressive form bei *be*), was shopping (1)
78. was sunbathing (1/4)
79. picked (schnell), drove, brought (Folgehandlungen)
80. were talking, broke (3)
81. were playing (4)
82. was reading, knocked (3)
83. were walking, fell, hurt (3)
84. were wearing, met (3)
85. was swimming, heard (3), was, was watching, thought (Folge: der daraufhin dachte), was
86. met, was riding (3)
87. were talking, was (3)
88. were watching, was listening (2)
89. was paying, broke (3) (schnell), stole (Folgehandlung)
90. were building, was surfing (2)
91. were having breakfast, was reading (2)
92. was writing, was making (2)
93. was tidying up, rang , told (3)
94. was doing, entered (3)
95. was packing, was helping (2)
96. was standing, took (kurz) (3)
97. was raining, got (3)
98. were living, broke (3)
99. were sitting, saw (3)
100. was playing, came (3)
101. were having, heard (3)
102. was doing, asked (3)
103. was repairing, was ironing (2)
104. was having, arrived (3)
105. were waiting, arrived (3)
106. was playing, was working, was repairing (drei gleichzeitige Handlungen, 2)
107. were having, set (3)
108. was leaving (gerade dabei war, wegzugehen) rang (3), had to (von *must* gibt es keine Dauerform)
109. was shaving, cut (3)
110. was bleeding, took (Folgehandlung: daraufhin brachte sie ihn ins Spital)
111. was playing, was listening (2)
112. stole, was swimming (3)
113. was walking, blew (3)
114. was having (4)
115. were they doing, were playing (4)
116. were spending (4)
117. was cooking, burnt/burned (3)
118. was watering, hurt (3)
119. saw, was sitting, was listening (2/3)
120. came, were having (3) / came, had (zwei Folgehandlungen: er kam und dann hatten wir Tee)
121. was having (4)
122. wanted, asked (Folgehandlungen) (*want* steht nicht in der progressive form)
123. were walking, began (3)
124. were waiting, ran (3)
125. fell, was painting (3)
126. was reading, heard (3), got, looked (zwei Folgehandlungen), was crying (2) (sie hat bereits geschrien)
127. was having, exploded (3)
128. was doing, slipped, crashed (3)
129. took (schnell), wasn't looking (3)
130. saw, was wearing (3)

131. had to (keine progressive form bei *must*),
 was barking (4)
132. was (keine progressive form bei *be*)
133. came, showed (zwei Folgehandlungen: sie kam und dann zeigten wir ihr ...)
134. were talking (1)
135. was having, was burning (2)
136. was studying (4)
137. were picking, was getting (2)
138. was watching, dropped (3)

page 89

1. have had to
2. has been able to
3. Has she been allowed to
4. have not been able to (have been unable to)
5. haven't had to
6. has not been allowed to
7. has had to, has not been allowed to
8. have not been able to (have been unable to)
9. Have you been able to

pages 90, 91

1. Have you been (*yet*) (☺ II / p68),
 was (*yesterday*) (☺ I / p76,77)
2. is going to wear (persönl. Plan) (☺ II p47)
3. met (*ago*) (☺ I / p76,77)
4. have had to (*for*) (☺ II / p68,p89)
 am, is (*now*)
5. are going to buy (persönl. Plan) (☺ II / p47)
6. will be (☺ II / p45,46),
 are going to have (persönl. Plan) (☺ II / p47)
7. are bringing (*look*) (☺ I / p51,52)
8. have *already* posted (☺ II / p68)
9. have not been able to / have been unable to
 (☺ II / p68,p89)
10. have *already* done (☺ II / p68),
 may/ are allowed to (☺ II / p6,7)
11. are the boys doing, are watching (☺ I / p51,52)
12. have done, have broken (☺ II / p68)
 am, am going to buy (☺ II / p47)
13. calls, phones (☺ II / p88)
14. did you last see (*when*) (☺ I / p76,77)
 think, met, was (*last*) (☺ I / p76,77)
15. was (*ago*) (☺ I p 76/77)
16. are you going to spend (☺ II / p47),
 went (*last*) (☺ I / p76,77),
 are going to fly (☺ II / p47),
 have not been (*for ages*) (☺ II / p68)
17. has never been (☺ II / p68),
 is going (☺ I / p82, Merke)
18. visited, was (*yesterday*) (☺ I / p76,77)
19. won't be (☺ II / p45,46),
 have studied (Resultat: er wird für uns nicht schwer sein) (☺ II / p68)
20. has snowed (Resultat: die Straßen sind weiß)
 (☺ II / p68), are

21. is still snowing (*look*) (☺ I / p51,52),
 are going to make (☺ II / p47)
22. Do you often see, meet (☺ I / p50),
 have not seen (*for ages*) (☺ II / p68)
23. Did you often see, met, was (☺ I / p76,77)
24. are, has not rained (*for*) (☺ II / p68),
 will rain (*hope*) (☺ II / p45,46)
25. has finished, is (Resultat: she is happy now)
 (☺ II / p68)
26. has not been able to / has been unable to (*for*)
 (☺ II / p68,p89), is still sitting (☺ I / p51,52)
27. won't be allowed to, will have to (☺ II / p6,7)
28. will be (☺ II / p45,46)
29. will have / 'll have (☺ II / p45,46)
30. is sleeping, is jumping (☺ I / p51,52) or was sleeping, was jumping (☺ II / p79)
31. go (☺ II /p88)
32. is going to be, are going to have (☺ II / p47)
33. are you knitting (*now*) (☺ I / p51,52),
 were knitting (☺ II / p79)
34. gets (☺ II / p88), is going to buy (☺ II / p47)
35. have *never* drunk (☺ II / p68),
 will never try (*think*) (☺ II / p45,46)
36. didn't smoke (*last*) (☺ I / p76,77),
 will *probably* give up (☺ II / p45,46)
37. were you doing (☺ II / p79),
 called, prepared, took (Folgehandlungen mit past simple)
38. have had to (☺ II / p68,p89),
 know (☺ I / p52 *Ausnahmen*), will enjoy (*hope*)
 (☺ II / p45,46)

SMILE
Grammar

ISBN 978-3-7074-1306-9

ISBN 978-3-7074-1307-6

ISBN 978-3-7074-1308-3

ISBN 978-3-7074-1309-0

SMILE ist bei LehrerInnen, SchülerInnen und Eltern die beliebteste Lern- und Übungsreihe für Englisch, denn:

- Jeder Band ist genau auf das entsprechende Lernjahr und den österreichischen Lehrplan abgestimmt.
- Jedes Kapitel enthält eine übersichtliche Zusammenstellung der Regeln sowie viele Übungsbeispiele zum jeweiligen Stoffgebiet.
- Vokabeln können im "Words"-Teil am Ende des Buches nachgeschlagen werden.
- Mit dem "Key", dem Lösungsteil, kann man leicht überprüfen, ob man fehlerfrei gearbeitet hat.
- Dieser "Key" bietet nicht nur die richtige Lösung, sondern auch Hinweise auf die entsprechenden Grammatikregeln. So kann man leicht feststellen, warum die Lösung so und nicht anders lauten muss.

www.ggverlag.at

SMILE
READING COMPREHENSIONS

Schulbuchnummer 165678
ISBN 978-3-7074-1354-0

Schulbuchnummer 170669
ISBN 978-3-7074-1508-7

Schulbuchnummer 170670
ISBN 978-3-7074-1624-4

ISBN 978-3-7074-1846-0

Im modernen Englisch-Unterricht wird auf das Verständnis von Texten großer Wert gelegt, schon ab dem ersten Lernjahr! Konzentration und Aufmerksamkeit sind gefragt, um das Gelesene verstehen und Inhalte verwerten zu können.

- Bedachtnahme auf die **verschiedenen Arten von Leseverständnis**: **schnelles** Lesen (skimming / scanning) einerseits, **detailgenaues** Lesen (careful reading) andererseits.

- **Verschiedenste Textsorten, praxisbezogen und abwechslungsreich:** Dialog, Anweisung, Rezept, Einladung, Artikel, Wetterbericht, Geschichte, Fernsehprogramm, E-Mail, Brief, Gedicht, Interview etc.

- Möglichkeit der Selbstkontrolle am Ende des Werkes (**Key**).

www.ggverlag.at

SMILE
LISTENING COMPREHENSIONS

ISBN 978-3-7074-1978-8

ISBN 978-3-7074-2061-6

ISBN 978-3-7074-2184-2

ISBN 978-3-7074-2187-3

Verstehen, was in einer fremden Sprache gesprochen wird – das ist ein großes Thema im aktuellen Fremdsprachenunterricht Schon ab dem 1. Lernjahr muss das Hörverständnis trainiert werden!

Smile Listening Comprehensions bietet zu den einzelnen Hörbeispielen zahlreiche Übungen, die zeigen, ob die Schülerin / der Schüler den gehörten Text verstanden und sich gemerkt hat:

- Einfüllübungen
- True/False-Entscheidungen
- Aus mehreren vorgegebenen Lösungen die passende auswählen und vieles mehr

www.ggverlag.at